BOOK by BOOK

THE COMPLETE GUIDE TO CREATING
MOTHER-DAUGHTER BOOK CLUBS

CINDY HUDSON

SEAL PRESS

Here's to moms and daughters reading together!!

Cindy Hudson

4773 7696 4/12

Book by Book
The Complete Guide to Creating Mother-Daughter Book Clubs

Copyright © 2009 by Cindy Hudson

Published by
Seal Press
A Member of the Perseus Books Group
1700 Fourth Street
Berkeley, California

ISBN: 978-1-58005-299-3

Library of Congress Cataloging-in-Publication Data

Hudson, Cindy, 1960-
  Book by book : the complete guide to creating mother-daughter book clubs / by Cindy Hudson.
      p. cm.
  Includes index.
  1. Book clubs (Discussion groups) 2. Group reading. 3. Mothers and daughters--Social networks. I. Title.
  LC6619.H83 2009
  367--dc22
                                    2009018099

9 8 7 6 5 4 3 2

Cover design by Kate Basart, Union Pageworks
Interior design by Megan Jones Design
Printed in the United States of America by Maple-Vail
Distributed by Publishers Group West

To Madeleine, Catherine and Randy,
whose love and support make all my efforts possible.

And to my mom,
who first ignited my passion for books.

TABLE of CONTENTS

INTRODUCTION

WHEN I STARTED my first mother-daughter book club with my daughter Madeleine, books were already a passion for us. We had read together since she was born, and when her sister, Catherine, came along a few years later, reading together offered a way for Madeleine and me to have some time just for the two of us. Soon I began to make time to read to Catherine on her own as well, and sometimes we would choose a family book that my husband, Randy, or I would read out loud to everyone.

Even though we continued to make reading a priority in our house as the girls started school, I noticed in fourth grade that some of Madeleine's friends labeled reading "uncool." I wanted to find a way to keep it fun for her, and I also felt the need to connect socially with other moms. There never seemed to be enough time to get together with other women whose daughters were the same ages as mine. I also thought a mother-daughter book club would let me combine the fun of reading with my daughter and the opportunity to get to know other moms and their daughters. Fortunately, I found a kindred spirit in Madeleine's Girl Scout troop leader, Karen Gotting. Karen had also been mulling over the idea of starting a book club, and we decided to begin one together. We each asked several moms to join us, eventually ending up with a group of six mother-daughter pairs.

Madeleine and I loved discovering books through our book club that we never would have found on our own. While we didn't like every selection we read, we could often appreciate books we didn't like after we'd talked about them in the group. Book club became something we looked forward to every month.

Three years after I created this club with Madeleine, Catherine let me know she was ready to be in a mother-daughter book club of her own. This time I joined with my dear friend Ellen Saunders, and each of us invited other moms. As with Madeleine's club, our goal was to expand our connection to the community by bringing in mothers and daughters we hadn't known before, and again we ended up with six pairs. While our experience in this new club mirrored that of my first one in many ways, this group had its own personality—we chose different books to read, had different ideas for activities outside of book club, and focused on different things in our discussions.

As the girls grew and started middle school, then high school, the books we read and the issues we tackled challenged us in unexpected ways. We ended up talking about many topics we'd never envisioned discussing when our girls were in elementary school, including underage drinking, date rape, deciding whether to have sex with a boyfriend, teen pregnancy and parenthood, and many other types of risky behavior. We also read books that were laugh-out-loud funny, told tales of fantastical worlds, and relayed true stories about people and events.

When looking back over the long tenure of both my clubs, I realize we have accomplished even more than we hoped to when we started out. We have created a community of moms and daughters who share much more than a reading list. We have been there to cheer each other on, help each other through tough times, and contribute in some small but important way to raising each other's daughters. We have imparted our values and beliefs through book discussions, and we have had a lot of fun in the process.

Our groups have changed to accommodate the girls' evolving schedules and needs over the years, and now we are on the cusp of change again. The girls in Catherine's book club are in high school, and those in Madeleine's all plan to be in college during the fall of 2009. For the last year we have been very aware of the fleeting moments we have left together, and we are determined to find a way to continue meeting even after the girls leave home. Our connections are too strong at this point to let them fade away.

I passionately believe that mother-daughter book clubs help us stay connected with our daughters and build lasting relationships with other people as well. These groups are capable of changing your life in ways you can't imagine when you are just beginning to consider organizing your first meeting. I wrote this book to help you answer the questions you will have as you put your group together, and as you build your club in the years that follow. My advice comes foremost from my own experience and that of the moms and daughters in my two book clubs. It also comes from moms across the country who are as passionate about their mother-daughter book clubs as I am about mine. You will hear their voices as they share stories about books they have read, challenges they have faced, and other activities they have scheduled. This book is richer because of their input.

FOREWORD

I MET CINDY, HER daughter, and a handful of other members of her book club in Portland last year. All of them had come to a reading I did at a local bookstore. I'd exchanged a few emails with Cindy prior to the meeting, so I knew a little about her website and her interest in spreading the word about mother-daughter book clubs.

What impressed me most about that evening was not Cindy and her dynamism—although she is definitely a dynamic person. What impressed me were the girls—the daughters in her mother-daughter book club. Each girl had such strongly held opinions; each had cultivated the ability to think critically about books. I'm certain these girls would have been an impressive crowd if they hadn't been mother-daughter book club members, but it seemed to me that the experience of discussing books together on a regular basis had enlivened, emboldened, and enriched them. When I met those girls, I thought to myself, *That's what I want for my daughter.*

My daughter, Kai, is just turning ten, and she and I have been in a mother-daughter book club for two and a half years. In that time I've noticed some real changes in our book club girls. They are bolder, more self-assured, more discriminating about the books we read, and more precise in their observations. Some of this is, of course, due to maturation—but not all of it.

When we started our group, our daughters were seven. We didn't really have a plan, but two of the moms in the triumvirate that initiated the club were in book clubs with their older daughters, so they had a lot of good ideas about how to run our own. Even so, we soon discovered that some of what worked in the other clubs didn't work in ours. We arrived at our format largely through trial and error. That's why I think this book provides a real service to moms organizing their own book clubs. What Cindy presents to you in these pages is not one formula for a successful book club, but many ideas about how to tailor the club to the needs of the individuals in your group.

Though my daughter is a terrific reader, I still read our book club books out loud to her. Every night, we locate our favorite fuzzy pink pillows, I pour two glasses of lemonade, Kai gets our snack, and we curl up together to read. It is one of the most enjoyable parts of my day. When we have finished our book club selection for the month, we still have this time together, but usually then we each read our own book. While reading side by side is nice, there's something special about experiencing the same book at the same time. Without the commitment to the club, I don't think the reading out loud would happen as consistently as it now does.

Last week I spoke at my daughter's school. After the presentation, three of the book club girls came up to me. They wanted to know what I thought about this month's book club selection. They couldn't wait until book club day to discuss it . . . and you know what? I can't wait either. I enjoy the discussion as much as the girls do.

—Gennifer Choldenko

NEWBERY HONOR AUTHOR OF *AL CAPONE DOES MY SHIRTS*

Part 1

A NEW CHAPTER: HOW TO GET YOUR CLUB STARTED

1

WHY BE IN A MOTHER-DAUGHTER BOOK CLUB?

" My daughter can learn from the experiences of other moms, and I can learn from the point of view of other daughters. And I think when we are at book club, we all see our family members a little more as human beings and not just as our mom or daughter. I watch other mothers affirm or question my daughter's perspectives. She sees other kids listen to her mom. And the amazing thing about books, of course, is the whole of human experience is right there, ready for us to share in it together. "

—Joan Overholser
PORTLAND, OREGON

UNEXPECTED BENEFITS

ASK ANY MOM why she's in a mother-daughter book club with her daughter, and she's likely to give you an answer that's slightly different from that of any other mom you ask. There are many benefits to being in a mother-daughter book club. Some are tangible, like increasing your daughter's reading skills, while others are harder to quantify, such as keeping a close bond with your daughter as she grows.

You probably already have your own, very specific reasons why you want to create a book club with your daughter. They may include some or all of the following:

- Enhancing your daughter's reading skills
- Staying connected with your daughter as she grows
- Nurturing your daughter's self-confidence
- Helping your daughter learn life skills
- Spending social time with other moms/girls
- Building a community of caring friends

It is likely the group you form will come to fulfill many of your expectations, but be prepared to be surprised, and challenged, by your experience in ways you never imagined. Any club you create will be dynamic, changing over the years as all of your members create your group together. Even though your members may have much in common, you will probably all focus on different aspects of your group that are most important to you.

Let's take a look at each of the major benefits listed above in more detail. Quotes from moms in my own two book clubs show that each person in a book club may place more importance on one benefit over another.

Enhancing Your Daughter's Reading Skills

❝ When we were first asked to join the book club, my primary motivation for saying yes was to encourage my daughter to learn to read more and to enjoy it. I'm happy to say that has happened. But what I also ended up gaining was a group of wonderful friends and experiences with precious memories of growing together. ❞

—Janelle Asai

❝ Mother-daughter book club discussions help the girls learn how to identify and discuss underlying themes of a book. Developing confidence in this task is helpful during high school and college years. ❞

—Karen Berson

Bonnie Lash Freeman, director of training and special projects for the National Center for Family Literacy, in Louisville, Kentucky, says a parent's reading with a child can stimulate two things:

- Motivation to learn to read and to continue reading
- Expansion of vocabulary

"Kids are always watching what you do," says Freeman. "If they see you pick up a book and read, they are more likely to want to read, too. They can also learn more vocabulary because the words in books are different than the words we speak. When you read to your children you can stop and explain words they don't understand, or talk about other words they know that may mean the same thing."

According to the "Kids & Family Reading Report" released recently by Scholastic, "high frequency readers are more likely to have positive self-perceptions and to associate strong reading skills with future success." It also concludes that "parents' reading behaviors are likely to have the greatest impact on kids' involvement with books." Yet the study finds that the number of kids actually reading for fun drops off after age eight.

Being in a mother-daughter book club provides a way for moms to model good reading behavior for their daughters and help them continue to see reading for fun and pleasure as important throughout their lives.

Staying Connected with Your Daughter As She Grows

" Our mother-daughter book club plays a large role in the incredible bond I have with my daughter. Book discussions helped us develop an easy, communicative relationship, encouraging candid dialogue that I cherish . . . and we've had fun together. "

—Karen Gotting

" A mother-daughter book club is more about the mother-daughter part than about 'book' or 'club.' You can read a book on your own, but it's something special to talk about it, argue about it, and share the experience with your daughter. You may even learn something about each other. I guarantee you moments when your daughter's perspective and insights will fill you with awe and pride. "

—Jan Ohman

If you start your mother-daughter book club when your daughter is seven or eight, you may feel as though the two of you share a special bond that will last forever. While that may be true, many girls begin to pull away from their parents, especially their moms, as they near adolescence. They may want to spend less and less time with their moms and more and more time with their peers. Being in a mother-daughter book club won't prevent that from happening entirely, but it can give you a regularly scheduled activity that opens up dialogue between you and your daughter on important issues.

Even if you begin your group when your daughter is older and already busy with friends and outside activities, book club can give you a way to find quiet moments in the day when you connect one-on-one to read together or talk about what you are reading.

Nurturing Your Daughter's Self-Confidence

" A mother-daughter book club meeting is a safe place for girls
to voice their opinions, especially when those opinions differ
from others' in the group. They learn to be comfortable talking
with the moms in the club, as well as with the other girls. It is
so gratifying to watch their confidence grow as they come to
see themselves as valuable members of the group."

—Ellen Saunders

In many ways, a girl is likely to see her own mom and the other
moms in the group as experts on many topics. Younger girls
in particular are likely to see moms as authority figures they
must defer to. That's why the mothers in a group, in particular, can help nurture girls' self-confidence by really listening to
what they have to say, and by acknowledging when they learn
something from a girl's comment or consider a new perspective
on an issue being discussed. This type of support can help the
daughters see themselves as having valuable opinions that influence others.

Helping Your Daughter Learn Life Skills

" I've enjoyed the mother-daughter book club especially because
my daughter is a typical teenager, and she's not very communicative. So the book discussions help us to connect with each
other, as well as the other moms and daughters, since she's
more talkative with her peers than with me."

—Lisa Willke

From giving speeches in school to negotiating with friends on the
playground, your daughter benefits when she can communicate
well. Yet being able to express what you think is an important

life skill that many of us—including many moms—have difficulty mastering. Speaking up in a group that is sure to be made up of many different types of personalities is also a good skill to nurture. Mother-daughter book club provides a safe environment where you can practice articulating your thoughts and communicating them.

Plus, when you host book club periodically, you also get the chance to talk with your daughter about planning for a social event. By working together to choose a book for everyone to read and preparing food and drinks for everyone in your group, you help your daughter learn social skills that she can use in other venues as well.

Spending Social Time with Other Moms/Girls

" I've found the socializing/dinner aspect just as rewarding as the book reading and discussion. Since our daughters are all in the same grade, it has been comforting to compare and contrast experiences of our parenting/daughter milestones. Bottom line, it's been a pleasure to watch these young girls grow into accomplished young women within the closer lens of a book club . . . all because I love to read!"

—Yasmeen Nazeeri

Moms and daughters both benefit from the separate social time they may have with their peers at a mother-daughter book club meeting. With all the demands of work, home life, and kids' activities, moms often don't make time to socialize with other moms unless it's at the soccer field or a school event. Yet unstructured social time is where moms are more likely to share information related to child rearing, talk about concerns they have about work or family life, or find out about community events. This opportunity to relax and chat can also be a much-needed break from everyday stress.

When girls have their own social time at book club, they have the chance to relate differently to each other than they do in the classroom, on the playground, or on the sports field. Seeing each other in a neutral setting where there are fewer expectations to perform may help them work through difficulties they have with each other elsewhere. It also helps them build social skills of their own without the constraints of adults watching over them.

Building a Community of Caring Friends

" When I was asked about joining a group, I was recently widowed, and my older children were away at college. I thought, *Oh, how awesome—a place where we can be like all the other family groups, just moms and daughters.* Although I am aware statistically that there are many single parents all over the place, it just so happens that my daughter and I didn't know very many at all, so we felt 'different.' This was a place we didn't feel so much that way.**"**

—Joan Overholser

" I love being in a mother-daughter book club for the opportunities to read the same books my daughter reads, to share my experiences, feelings, and thoughts with moms and daughters from diverse backgrounds on a wide range of topics. The book club has given me a second chance to grow up through a different lens.**"**

—Show-Ling Shyng

When you are starting out, you have no idea of the life challenges and rewards outside of book club that you may experience through the years. Your book club moms and girls may play very important roles in helping you through any rough spots that come along, as well as celebrating important milestones with you.

In my clubs we have given each other advice and comfort about caring for elderly parents, supported each other through our own health issues, and shored each other up through many mundane, everyday struggles. We have also cheered for our members at plays and choir concerts, and through other successes large and small. When you create a mother-daughter book club, you create the opportunity to build your own community that will see you through life's ups and downs over the years.

BEING ABLE TO TALK ABOUT TOUGH ISSUES BROUGHT UP IN BOOKS

" I'm in two mother-daughter book clubs with my two daughters, and I just finished reading *Nineteen Minutes* by Jodi Picoult for my youngest daughter's book club. I would have never read this book on my own, and when I first picked it up, I was groaning and whining about it. It is a story about people in high school and a high school shooter. As I read, though, I realized what a great discussion we would have with our sophomore daughters about the characters and issues the book brings up, like bullying, peer pressure, and isolation. This is what it is really about, isn't it? Having the venue to discuss really hard issues with your daughter. "

—Jayne Mitchell

IRLS MAY WANT more information about issues that worry them, but they don't know how to ask their moms the questions. Body changes, friends who say they don't like you

anymore, pressure to have sex or drink alcohol . . . all these concerns may be on a girl's mind. Talking about these experiences
as they happen to characters in a book is a safe way to broach
the subjects that you may both be reluctant to tackle head-on.

Moms and daughters also both benefit from hearing what
the other generation has to say about these issues. Even if you
discuss them at home, family dynamics may prevent you from
truly listening to what the other has to say. Mother-daughter
book club can provide a neutral environment that encourages
you to really hear each other, especially if other moms and girls
in the group express similar opinions.

THE OVERRIDING BENEFIT—HAVING A LOT OF FUN

OVER AND OVER again, when moms are asked why they are
in a mother-daughter book club, they mention how much
fun it is, in addition to all the other benefits they realize. Even
though you can expect many rewards, having fun at your meetings is what will keep making book club more of a treat than
a chore, and will keep making you return month after month,
year after year. In some ways, that makes this the most important benefit of all.

CREATE YOUR CLUB WITH THESE BENEFITS IN MIND

THE CHAPTERS THAT follow talk about how to create your
club, how to schedule enriching activities, and how to

meet challenges that are sure to pop up along the way. You will hear from other moms who have successfully started clubs and kept them going, as well as parenting experts, authors, and others with advice to share. As you read, you will find even more evidence to support the major benefits outlined here, and you will surely come across a few more fringe benefits as well.

Keep in mind all the advantages you want to achieve as you create a club that will work best for you and your daughter.

Reading Aloud to Your Daughter

When Madeleine and Catherine were babies, I loved holding their warm, snuggly bodies against me as I read picture books over and over to them. As they got older, I worried that some of the closeness we felt when we read together would disappear when they started to read on their own. Then I realized I didn't have to stop reading books to them just because they were capable of stringing words together without me. So we continued to snuggle up on the couch after school or in bed before the lights went out, and we had fun talking about the characters or situations in the books we chose.

As it turns out, there are also practical reasons for continuing to read to your daughter as she grows. Joanne Meier provides research guidance for Reading Rockets, an educational initiative that aims to inform and inspire parents and others on how to teach kids to read. She says that reading aloud "is a great opportunity to model for your child what good,

▶

fluent reading sounds like." She also advises that the best read-aloud books are a bit above the child's reading level.

"If they haven't achieved that level of fluency yet, it can be motivating and exciting for them. It really brings the book to life, and kids will sit rapt, chapter after chapter, because you are telling a story in a way they can't," Meier says.

How can you make sure your daughter will want you to continue reading aloud to her as she grows? Here are a few tips for making read-aloud time a great mother-daughter activity:

- Read with expression, and get into creating voices for the characters. You can even try on accents. If you read with a monotone voice, it will be easy for your daughter to tune out what you are saying and want to stop.

- Modulate your voice to go with the action. Slow down when something scary is about to happen, and speed up when the pace picks up.

- Pause when you want to talk about something. You can stop to laugh during a funny scene, or when you want to explain a situation your daughter may not be familiar with. You can even stop to cry if you are reading a particularly sad scene. Reacting to what you read gives the story meaning.

- Make reading time special. Cover up with a quilt or sip hot cocoa while you turn the pages together.

- Choose a good downtime, like when your daughter is having an after-school snack before she starts

▶ homework, or before bedtime. This way, you won't both be distracted by other activities.

- Don't make it a requirement. If you tell your daughter she has to sit with you and read for twenty minutes whether she wants to or not, it can set up a power struggle between the two of you. Reading together should be a welcome break you both look forward to, not a chore.

2
WHEN TO START A MOTHER-DAUGHTER BOOK CLUB

"I have most enjoyed talking at our meetings with the other moms and girls about everyone's feelings and thoughts about the stories. While Esther, my daughter, and I already had a very close relationship and actively communicate on a regular basis, it has been that much more fun for us to share with these other girls and their moms in a close environment. Our club is new, and we have a lot that we can improve upon, but I already see girls who were shy and introverted opening up with each new discussion meeting and story read. I hope we can continue on to see just what the girls (and even us moms) are capable of achieving together in the future!"

—Gina Davis
"BOOK CHICKS" MOTHER-DAUGHTER BOOK CLUB,
ST. PETERS, MISSOURI

FINDING THE RIGHT TIME

WHEN MY OLDEST daughter, Madeleine, was nine, I joined together with five other moms and their daughters to create my first mother-daughter book club. Madeleine and her friends were at a magical age. They were happy to have time set aside just for them and their moms each month, and they loved reading books. All of the girls were active with sports, music lessons, and other classes, but their homework load was light and their evenings were mostly free. We moms banded together for many reasons: We wanted to help our daughters learn to socialize, as well as to spend time socializing ourselves, we wanted to nurture the girls' love of reading, and we wanted to carve out time in our busy family lives that was just for us and our daughters.

Later, when deciding when to begin a second club with my younger daughter, Catherine, I had a chance to consider whether starting younger would be better. Ultimately, I decided that nine seemed like the right age for Catherine's book club girls, too. Since then, I have learned of moms in clubs across the country who successfully started clubs when their daughters were every age from seven to twelve or older. What time you decide to create your own club will depend on many factors, including how old your daughter is when:

- You know you want to be in a club.
- Friends invite you to form a new club or join an existing one.
- You think your daughter is ready for the experience.
- Your situation in life allows you to set aside time for book club each month.

CAN A DAUGHTER BE TOO YOUNG OR TOO OLD?

I F YOU'VE KNOWN you want to be in a mother-daughter book club ever since your daughter was a toddler, you may wonder just how old she has to be before you can get started. Should she be reading on her own, or can you read the books to her? Will it be difficult to find other girls her age and their moms to join you?

On the other hand, if you have a daughter who is in middle school, you may also wonder if you've already missed your chance to be in a club. Your personal circumstances may not have allowed you to be in a club before, or else you may not have known anyone to create one with you. You believe both you and your daughter could benefit, and she's interested, too. Is it too late?

While there may be an "ideal" age for daughters to form book clubs with their moms, almost any age will work to start. Each age presents its own rewards and its own challenges, and if you and your daughter are both excited about being in a book club, you can always benefit from the time you spend with each other and with other moms and daughters who like to read.

AN IDEAL AGE

CATHERINE WEIGEL FOY, LCSW, LMFT, a clinical lecturer at the Weinberg School of Psychology and an affiliate therapist with the Family Institute, both at Northwestern University in Evanston, Illinois, believes that a good time to start a mother-daughter book club is as soon as girls are independent readers—around eight years old. Foy has been working with groups of moms and their nine- and ten-year-old daughters for more than ten years; she has also worked extensively with adolescents and their parents.

"It's a wonderful starting place, because girls are so open to influence from their moms when they are eight," says Foy. She adds that while eight may be ideal, she believes no age is "too old," and she advises moms that if the opening is acceptable to an adolescent daughter, they should "run with it."

How you create your club will differ depending on the age of the daughters when you start, and each stage will present its own goals, rewards, and challenges. Let's take a closer look at three distinct age groups—seven and eight, nine and ten, and eleven and twelve—to see what you may be able to expect from each.

CULTIVATING A LIFELONG LOVE OF READING WITH SEVEN- AND EIGHT-YEAR-OLDS

As Foy notes, a perfect time to start your mother-daughter book club may be when your daughter is eight, especially since girls that age are usually open to influence from their moms. "You're trying to help support their love of reading for enjoyment," says Foy. "They see that you enjoy the book, that you can talk about it, and they have a very positive experience with you overall."

Julie is in a mother-daughter book club that started when the girls were seven and eight, and she agrees that it was the best time for them to begin. "Some of the girls who weren't big readers had a fun reason to read," says Julie, which she believes helped make them stronger readers. "As a mother, I feel like I'm showing my daughter the importance of books, as well as the value of hearing others' ideas. I liked knowing that all the girls could read the book by themselves, even though some of the moms chose to read to them."

Book clubs with girls this age are more likely to be mom-driven than girl-driven. This means that you will probably suggest the books and decide which activities to schedule at meetings. You can give the girls more say in the process, and start to nurture their independence, by giving them choices from an acceptable list. For example, you can bring several books to suggest, then let the girls vote on which one they would prefer to read.

You may also find that when your girls are this young, it's harder for them to sit still for a lengthy book discussion. You can help keep them engaged during meetings by adding in games and crafts. Of course, this means you will probably spend more time planning your get-togethers, but you may be able to share those responsibilities with other moms in your group. Look for examples of games and crafts you can plan for your book club in Chapter 8.

BUILDING CONFIDENCE IN NINE- AND TEN-YEAR-OLDS

As I mentioned earlier, I started both of the mother-daughter book clubs I'm in with my daughters when the girls were nine and in fourth grade. For me, it seemed like the best time to begin for several reasons:

- The girls were reading books in school with more complicated plots, and they were expected to discuss them in class.

- While they both loved to read, some of their friends were saying that reading was "uncool," and I wanted to keep them reading for fun.

- I wanted to be in a social group with my daughters, an older version of the playgroups we had been part of when they were toddlers.

Foy says you're more likely to find confident readers in this age group. She believes this is also a good time for moms to help girls learn to be assertive with their opinions. "At this time, girls' thoughts often go inside," she explains. "They see things, but they don't speak them quite as frankly as they once did. Having a book club, where you're nurturing and want to know your daughter's opinions and thoughts, is a way to help her maintain her voice."

Girls this age are also likely to be nervous about what to expect socially when they enter middle school, even if they don't talk about it. If they are in a book club in which they read about characters older than they are, they have an entrée to talk about issues that may be worrying them. This is a good time to read books that delve into questions such as how your daughter should react if her friend stops wanting to be with her, or how it will feel for her to like a boy as more than a friend. It's often easier to talk about these topics before they come up in real life.

Daughters in this age group are likely to straddle the line between wanting to act more grown up and wanting to still be little kids. Just like younger girls, they will appreciate engaging in activities during book discussions.

TRANSITIONING INTO TEEN ISSUES WITH ELEVEN- AND TWELVE-YEAR-OLDS

IF YOU WERE not able to start a mother-daughter book club when your daughter was younger, there is still good reason to organize one now. Middle-school years may be especially difficult for some girls, and a book club can be an important outlet for them to talk about issues at school and hear opinions from their friends and other mothers.

Emma formed her book club when the girls were in sixth grade, after she noticed that her daughter's school progress reports noted she didn't participate much in class discussions. "Another mom and I had a conversation about how both of our girls were well liked by their classmates but were a bit on the shy side. They rarely spoke up in class without being asked, and even then they contributed little," she says.

Emma and her friend thought it would be helpful to create an environment where their daughters could practice speaking in a group, a place where it was safe to share what was on their minds. "We hoped they would build confidence, and even if they didn't participate willingly, perhaps when they were called on they would begin to contribute to a greater degree," Emma says.

Book clubs for girls this age also have significant social value, and Emma says she wishes they had started years earlier, because it has been so much fun.

The most difficult aspect of starting a club when your daughter is this age may be convincing her to go along with the plan. Conflict between mothers and daughters can often make their relationship difficult, and if the daughter isn't already settled in an established mother-daughter book club, she may reject the idea. Still, Foy says it's worth making the effort. In fact, she suggests that moms start reading to their adolescent daughters at bedtime if they are working to overcome problems between them. She says this simple act often connects to a good, positive memory from earlier childhood that can help bridge a relationship gap.

STARTING A CLUB IN THE FRINGE YEARS

YOU MAY WELL decide that you would really like to start your mother-daughter book club early, not wait until your daughter is eight. If that's the case, you will probably want to structure it less like a traditional book club, and more like a playdate or reading time at the library. You can have all your book club members gather and read a book out loud, then ask the girls to talk about what they've just heard. Throw in a few activities just for fun, and you've got a good foundation for transitioning into independent reading when your daughter is older.

What if your daughter is in high school? Is it too late then? Not if she wants to be in a book club with you. Foy says this is a good age for girls to hone their abstract-thinking skills, identify their own principles, and be more flexible when considering someone else's point of view. You can help your daughter develop these skills even more, which will serve her well when she leaves home for college and a career.

Tips for Working Moms

Don't despair about how you'll ever find time to be in a mother-daughter book club if you work full-time outside the home. Many of the moms in my mother-daughter book clubs, as well as those I hear from in clubs around the country, work full- or part-time, but that doesn't stop them from being able to enjoy reading books with their daughters and taking on hosting responsibilities when it's their turn. Working moms may have a few more balls to juggle, but by employing a few key strategies and a little preparation, they can minimize stress and reap all the advantages a mother-daughter book club offers.

- Get the book soon after it's assigned. Show-Ling works as a researcher at a public-health university, and her schedule requires her to travel and attend meetings frequently. Still, she's in two mother-daughter book clubs, and she says she has failed to finish a book only once. Her secret is to get a copy of the book as soon as possible and read every night before going to sleep.

- Make reading part of your mother-daughter time. Many moms read book club selections to their daughters. This allows you to connect with each other about the book outside of book club, spend time together, and make sure you finish reading by the time your meeting comes up.

- Simplify your meal preparations. While Jayne, who is a nurse-practitioner, often cooks meals from scratch for book club, she doesn't hesitate to order pizza

▶

when she's pressed for time. Determine what your fallback meals will be when it's your turn to host. If you serve snacks instead of meals, have a handy list in your head of healthy snacks that take little time to prepare.

- Enlist your daughter's help. Depending on her age, she may be able to contribute to food preparation or housecleaning before you host a meeting at your home. Giving her responsibilities also helps her feel more a part of the group, and lets her know what it takes to prepare for social events.

- Let go of any expectations of being perfect. You probably don't expect to walk into a squeaky-clean environment and be served a gourmet meal when you show up for book club meetings at the homes of other members of your group. Assume that other members are giving you the same leeway.

- If at all possible, ask for a regular meeting date. Janelle, who often traveled for work as a nutritionist, said it was easier to make sure she would be in town for book club when she knew it would be on the third Thursday of each month. With that date in mind, she could schedule out-of-town trips for different times.

- Enlist help from others. Do you need someone to look after a younger sibling when you attend book club meetings? See if a neighborhood baby sitter is willing to work with you on a regular basis. Do you have dif-ficulty getting home to pick up your daughter before you head to your meeting? Ask someone else in your group to bring her, and drive to your meeting straight from work.

- Help others when you can. Be sure to offer help to other working moms in your club when you are able. If you routinely do favors for each other, you can each help lighten the load.

3
HOW BIG SHOULD YOUR CLUB BE?

" Being in a book group with my daughter gave me the opportunity to share my love of reading with her. We could gossip about the characters, talk about the choices they made, and discuss whether or not we would have made the same choices. It didn't really matter whether we liked the book or not. It gave me a real window into her world, and a chance to share my values and thoughts with her. "

—Wendie Lubic
WASHINGTON, D.C.

THIS CLUB FITS ME JUST RIGHT

LIKE GOLDILOCKS FINDING the "just right" bed size in the home of the three bears, you want to find the just-right club size for you. While Goldilocks found her perfect fit through trial and error, it will be easier for you in the long run if you put thought into what the right size for your mother-daughter book club is before you ask people to join. But how will you know what size is best for you?

LOOK FOR OTHER GROUP EXAMPLES

ARE YOU IN a book club with other adults? Is your daughter in a Girl Scout troop? Are you working on a project with a group of people at the office? Are you part of a prayer group at church? When you start thinking about other groups, both large and small, that you're already a member of, you can begin to notice and consider the advantages and disadvantages of each. Both of my mother-daughter book clubs have twelve people—six moms and six daughters—and that feels just right for me. Here's a look at some of the pros and cons of different club sizes to help you decide what's just right for you.

A SMALL CLUB WORKS BEST FOR ME

HOW SMALL IS a small club? I identify it as having anywhere from four to eight members, or two to four mother-daughter pairs. Smaller groups offer several advantages. For one, it's easier to host a small group. If your book club meeting is at your house and you're expecting just one or two other moms and daughters to arrive, you probably won't have to worry about whether you have enough soup bowls or plates to go around. You'll also have plenty of room to spread out when you gather to discuss the book, and picking a date for your next meeting will be easier if you have fewer schedules to consult. Hosting logistics aside, there are other reasons why a small group may appeal to you.

- Fewer people means more time for each person to talk about the book.

- A more intimate gathering may encourage more openness among members when talking about difficult or embarrassing topics.

- Group bonding may be easier if there are fewer people in the mix.

Show-Ling is in two mother-daughter book clubs—one small and one medium. She says it's easier to schedule meetings for her small group of four moms and four daughters, which is important to the moms in that group who work full-time. The biggest difference Show-Ling sees between her two clubs is the amount of social time each offers: "When Kyra and I meet with our mother-daughter book club, we have plenty of time to talk and socialize in addition to discussing the book."

A SMALL CLUB IS TOO SMALL FOR ME

EVEN IF YOU typically enjoy being with fewer people and have difficulty expressing your opinion in group settings, you may still decide that eight or fewer members are not enough for your book club. You may think so because:

- You'll be hosting and choosing books more often.

- Members may feel it's easier to reschedule with a small group and will allow other events to take precedence.

- With a smaller number of readers comes less variety in opinions and insights, so discussions may be less in-depth. Indeed, Show-Ling says she's noticed that having fewer mom-daughter pairs in her small book club means that "the book discussion may not be as interesting in terms of diversity of opinions."

A MEDIUM CLUB IS WHAT I'M LOOKING FOR

A MEDIUM-SIZE MOTHER-DAUGHTER BOOK club will have anywhere from ten to twelve members, or five to six mother-daughter pairs. Logistics get a little more difficult at this size but for the most part are still manageable. Even so, more consideration needs to go into hosting decisions, such as when and where you will meet. (See Chapter 5 for more information on this topic.) What are some of the advantages of forming a medium-size club?

- You'll probably read a greater variety of genres, since having more people usually equals broader interests.

- Your discussions will be more varied because more moms and daughters will be contributing their thoughts to the conversation.

- You can expand your social network and general awareness of different lifestyles by having more people to connect with.

As I noted earlier, both of my mother-daughter book clubs have twelve members. One of my favorite parts of our get-togethers is gathering for dinner before we sit down to discuss the book. The moms all sit together in one room, and the daughters sit together at a separate table in another room. In the moms' room, we catch up on each other's lives, discuss what's happening with the girls at school, and hear about issues going on at work or at home. Sometimes we even talk about the book and what subjects we think are most likely to come up when we join with the girls to discuss it.

I really like the variety of life situations in both of my groups: There are women who work full-time, work part-time, and stay home with their children. We come from different areas of the country and the world. We share recipes and advice about dentists and pediatricians and new restaurants to try. It's not surprising that we usually run out of time before we run out of things to talk about, and I would miss the interaction with such a diverse group of women if my clubs were smaller.

A MEDIUM CLUB IS TOO SMALL (OR TOO LARGE) FOR ME

ONE SIZE CERTAINLY doesn't fit all, and what I describe as a medium-size book club, even though it's the right size for me, has disadvantages you may want to consider as well.

- There's less time overall for each person to say what she thinks about issues in the book, which could be frustrating during discussions.

- Conversely, with more members it's easier for some people to feel uncomfortable speaking up and saying what they think about the book or a topic you've read about. So you may find that some members do most of the talking, while you seldom hear from others.

- More members means a wider range of preferences for certain types of books, so you may find yourself reading fantasy or nonfiction biographies, or some other genre you're not very fond of, more often than you'd like.

Of course, having more members also increases the likelihood of scheduling conflicts, particularly if your girls are involved in lots of after-school activities. That means you may have to accept that you won't attend all your book club meetings, and when you do go, you may not see everyone else. Our rule is that four out of six moms and daughters must be able to attend before we book a date.

A LARGE CLUB IS WHAT I'M LOOKING FOR

LARGE MOTHER-DAUGHTER book clubs have fourteen or more members, or seven or more mother-daughter pairs. More commonly, you'll find groups of this size organized by librarians or created from the entire list of girls in a classroom. Meetings are often held on a set date each month. That way, it's easier for moms and daughters to schedule other events around the regular book club date. Here's what you may appreciate about a large club:

- You will most likely hear a multitude of opinions that will help generate a lively book discussion.

- You can greatly expand your social network and get to know other moms and daughters you might otherwise have little contact with.

- There's less pressure to attend a meeting if a conflict comes up, because you know the meeting is likely to have enough people for a good dialogue.

Julie was in a mother-daughter book club with eight moms and eight daughters in Brookfield, Wisconsin. It was one of the largest clubs I've heard of, but Julie says she really liked having a large group, because it was easy to split responsibilities. "One mom-daughter pair hosted and provided food, and another planned the discussion game and provided small prizes," she says, noting that meetings were easier for the host team that way. Julie also liked that her group was big enough that there was always a core group available to get together, even if one or two families couldn't attend.

A LARGE CLUB IS TOO BIG FOR ME

WHAT ARE SOME of the challenges you may face if your group has fourteen or more members?

- You may find it harder to form deeper connections with one another, because you don't have enough time at meetings to get to know one another well.
- You may have to add more structure to your meetings to make sure everyone who wants to talk about the book has a chance to be heard.
- The logistics of where to meet and whether you will serve food become more challenging, particularly if you never know how many members may show up on any given book club date.

Julie acknowledged that one of the downsides of having a large club is that it's "harder to give everyone the chance to participate in the discussion." Her group came up with an innovative solution to make it work: "The mother and daughter who planned the discussion put prepared questions in an envelope that was passed around to the girls. Each girl selected a discussion question, gave her thoughts on the answer, and then opened the floor to discussion with others. That way, each girl was given the opportunity to lead a discussion."

BUILDING THE RIGHT CLUB FOR YOU

AS YOU CAN see, any size club you decide to form will have pluses as well as minuses. To make sure you form the size that's just right for you, you must consider those pluses and minuses carefully. Think about what may be most important to you, and what you may be willing to let slide. If you're working with another mom or two to form a club, talk it over with them before you move on to deciding who to invite, which is covered in the next chapter. Keep in mind that it's easier to increase the number of members in your group if you start small and want to grow larger than it is to decrease the number if you're unhappy being in a larger group.

Dads Are Important To Mother-Daughter Book Clubs, Too

When I was talking to Jayne's husband, Kevin, about this book, he told me, "Don't forget about the dads. They play a very important role in any mother-daughter book club." Of course, he was right. Getting buy-in from the dads of your mother-daughter pairs will go a long way toward helping your club be successful. What can dads do to help?

Depending on the age of your daughter and whether or not you have other children, dads can:

- Entertain your other children and get their dinner while you and your daughter attend a book club meeting.

▶

- Listen in as you read a book club choice to your daughter, so your whole family can discuss the book.

- Help you get ready when the meeting is hosted at your house, and pitch in on cleanup after everyone leaves.

- Be willing to take charge of the household if you go away for the weekend with your mother-daughter book club.

Even if you are no longer married to your daughter's father, he may be able to assist by caring for other siblings while you're at club meetings or when you go away for a weekend. The bottom line is, dads can be involved, too, and when they are, they reap benefits from your club as well:

- Having dad-only time with siblings when they plan a fun outing to a movie, a restaurant, or a local museum.

- Building a connection with their daughters by asking about the books they read for book club and talking about some of the issues that may come up during group discussion.

- Expanding their social network by getting to know some of the other dads and siblings of book club members.

When I'm getting ready for book club meetings at my house, I'm glad that I don't have to be stressed about what my husband, Randy, will do while we meet. Over the years, he's never complained about being banished to our bedroom for

▶

dinner or trying to keep quiet while we talk. When our daughters were younger and didn't have very much homework, he looked forward to having separate time with each girl while I was at a book club meeting with the other one. The time he spent with them alone helped him catch up each month on the important things going on in their lives. Kevin likens it to a looked-forward-to "forced date" with a sibling and says it's a good time to "go out and do something special during the week."

"The meeting itself may be limited to mothers and daughters," says Randy, "but we often extend the conversation around the family dinner table. Sometimes I'm jealous of the strengthening relationship between my wife and our daughters in their book clubs, and I like being as involved as I can."

And while dads shouldn't expect to participate in book discussions, they needn't be totally invisible on meeting nights. Show-Ling's husband, Bruce, pours wine for us on occasion, and Kevin has eaten dinner with the moms in our group. Randy says he likes to play the role of welcoming host and bartender, because it gives him "a chance to connect with friends of my wife and daughters before I'm exiled to another part of the house."

4
WHO TO INVITE

" Every time we get together for our book club meeting, everyone is so genuinely excited to be together—mothers and daughters. It brings me such pleasure to see my daughter so excited about a book and so eager to share her personal experiences with all our friends and with me. And I have developed strong bonds with the mothers from our book club. We're all genuinely curious about what we all think. "

—Maria Gallardo
WOODCLIFF LAKE, NEW JERSEY

MAKING CONNECTIONS

DECIDING WHO TO invite into your mother-daughter book club may be the toughest and most important decision you make. The mother-daughter pairs involved will contribute to your group's personality, influencing what types of books you read, determining where you hold your meetings, and ultimately affecting how long your group holds together. Maybe you already have some parameters for the types of moms and daughters you want to invite, or maybe you're worried about being labeled "exclusive" if you don't include anyone who wants to join.

Deciding who's going to be in your book club has the potential to cause a lot of stress, but it doesn't have to be that way. If you develop a clear understanding of what you want in a group, it will help you decide who will complement that vision.

MY STORY

I STARTED MY FIRST mother-daughter book club when Madeleine was in fourth grade. The club evolved from a conversation with Madeleine's Girl Scout leader, Karen. Karen's daughter, Kirsten, was an avid reader like Madeleine, and the two girls were friends. Karen and I wanted to strengthen their friendship and foster their love of reading, especially when we saw other girls the same age reject reading as "uncool." When we decided to move forward with our idea, we weren't sure at first who else would be in our club. How did we decide?

First off, we knew we didn't want to open our club up to all the girls in the same grade at our daughters' school. There were two classes of fourth graders, and roughly half of each class was made up of girls. The potential for a group that included more than twenty moms and twenty daughters was too overwhelming. We also decided against creating a club with all the Girl Scouts in the girls' troop, reasoning that it could create tensions in the troop if some girls didn't want to join.

After figuring out what we didn't want, Karen and I approached one of the fourth-grade teachers and asked her about girls who were reading at the same level as Kirsten and Madeleine. She recommended six other girls, which set us up for the possibility of a group of sixteen. But creating a group entirely from the girls' elementary school still didn't feel quite right to us. We didn't want to create the appearance of an exclusive subgroup of readers in the school, a group that wouldn't allow others in if they asked to join.

The more Karen and I thought about it, the more we realized we wanted to form a club that broadened our, and especially our daughters', connections to the community. So we decided that we would each ask one mom-daughter pair from school, and one pair we knew from different neighborhoods whose daughters attended different schools. We liked that all the girls wouldn't see each other at recess every day, and that our mother-daughter book club would be a place to forge friendships outside of our usual social connections.

FINDING WHAT WORKS FOR YOU

THE CLUB THAT Karen and I started eight years ago proved to be exactly what we were looking for. I liked the results so much that when I was putting together a club for my younger daughter, Catherine, three years later, I followed the same formula. In that case, I got together with my friend Ellen and her daughter Franny, and each of us invited two other mom-daughter pairs. After five years with a second club, I'm still happy with organizing a mother-daughter book club this way. However, I recognize that not everyone will choose to form a club like this. Creating the right club for you is key, and it's dependent on many factors, one being size, which we covered in Chapter 3. Since this chapter is about who to invite, let's explore what you're looking for: (a) Do you want to strengthen a group that already exists by giving it one more way to connect, or (b) Do you want to broaden your social circle?

STRENGTHENING AN EXISTING GROUP

LOOK AT ANY existing group that you and/or your daughter takes part in, and you'll find the potential to create a mother-daughter book club. Consider your daughter's classmates at school, a Girl Scout troop, a group of homeschooled students who share resources, a church group, members of a sports team, or even students in a community art class.

What are some of the reasons you may want to strengthen an existing group?

- More shared experiences will help members of the group grow closer.

- Group members may be able to overcome differences and learn more about each other when they see each other in a different context.

- If you already have fun being together, you may want to extend the time you spend as a group.

- It's easy to determine who you'll invite, because you'll want to include everyone who's already a member of the other group.

- Since everyone is included, no one can say you're exclusive.

Julie's daughter was in a relatively small seventh-grade class at school when some of the moms decided they wanted to form a mother-daughter book club. Sixteen girls were in the class, and the moms decided that if everyone wanted to join, they would probably form two groups. As it was, nearly half of the girls and their moms said yes, so they formed one large group. Soon after, one of the mom-daughter pairs who had said no because of other commitments asked if they could still join. Julie says, "They heard our discussions at school events and decided they were missing out."

You may decide strengthening an existing group is not the right approach for you, for one or more of the following reasons:

- Too much time together may be wearing on members of a group, and you risk creating more conflict if there's not enough time for girls to be apart.

- Inviting all the members of an existing group may make your book club larger than you'd like.

- If everyone feels pressured to join your book club, it could create resentment or a rift among members.

- You may have to deal with cliques in the club, just like the ones you find on the playground.

Think carefully before you decide to talk about your new mother-daughter book club in front of a group you're already involved with. Once you invite everyone to join, you can't change your mind, so know why you think this is a good idea before jumping in with both feet.

BROADENING YOUR SOCIAL CIRCLE

IF YOU'RE NOT part of an existing group that you want to create a club with, or if you would prefer to expand the number of people you and your daughter form relationships with, there are many other ways to create a new club. You could partner with another mom and daughter, like I did, with each of you asking mom-daughter pairs the other doesn't know. You can also put up a notice someplace you go regularly, such as the library, a community recreation facility, or your pediatrician's office. Another idea is to form a group from people you know casually who you'd like to get to know better.

What are some advantages of forming a mother-daughter book club with people who don't already know each other well?

- Members are more likely to join because they want to, not because they feel they have to.

- Your group is more likely to be diverse and bring new ideas to your discussions.

- It's fun to meet new people and get to know them better.

- You may forge close, lasting friendships.

When Catherine and I started our mother-daughter book club, we knew some of the moms and daughters, and some we met for the first time at our first meeting. Liza was one of the "new to us" girls; she went to a different elementary school from Catherine's. Two years later, Liza and Catherine were at the same middle school and they shared many of the same classes. Pretty soon they were calling each other every night to discuss homework and growing closer as friends in the process. Now, in high school, the girls cheer each other on at sports events, share test-taking tips, and attend social events as part of a group. Their friendship may very well not have developed if they hadn't first gotten to know each other in our mother-daughter book club.

There's always a downside to consider, and here's what you may find:

- Members of your new group may not have enough in common for you to bond well.

- It may take a long time for you to find enough people to form a group.

- Finding an easy place to meet may be harder if you don't live close to one another.

- Others may see your group as exclusive, a perception that could create social tensions in other areas of your life.

OTHER POINTS TO THINK ABOUT

DECIDING WHICH APPROACH is best for you will answer many, but not all, of your questions about who to invite. Other factors you should consider include the girls' ages and reading levels, and group homogeneity. Let's look at each of these details separately.

Age of the Girls

If you invite girls who are not all the same age, you should think about making the age range as narrow as possible and be prepared to make some tough decisions about what you'll read. It's obvious that a seven-year-old and a twelve-year-old will be at different reading levels and therefore be drawn to very different books. Yes, you can find books that will satisfy everyone in a broad age range like this one, but it's not easy to do month after month for years down the road.

Even if your girls fit a narrower age range—say, nine to twelve—you may find it difficult to choose books about subjects that appeal to all of them. Elementary school students and middle school students frequently see issues from differing perspectives, and the older girls may feel like the younger ones hold them back from reading and discussing books about characters facing more mature situations like the ones they encounter.

You're more likely to see mixed-age groups in libraries where a club may be organized for fourth and fifth graders, or for any student who's in middle school or high school. Even in instances like these, though, parents will often be confronted with what to do when their child "graduates" out of the group, or is impacted by the departure of someone else. Will your daughter be in the position of having to leave a group of people she's become close to? Is there another group of older girls she'll move into? It helps if you know the answers to these questions before these issues arise.

Reading Level

It's harder to know in advance what your girls' reading levels are, but they certainly play a role in the books you'll choose. If the reading level among girls is too broad, some will be frustrated because the books chosen are too challenging, while others will be frustrated because the books aren't challenging enough. It may be helpful, when extending an invitation, to include a list of books you may consider for the first year. You can acquire this list by looking at the books recommended in Appendix II, by talking to a youth librarian, or by asking your daughter's teacher. A mom and daughter who are invited can then anticipate what the book club holds in store and can decide for themselves if they want to join your group.

Group Homogeneity

The overriding commonality of some mother-daughter book clubs will be membership in an ethnic, social, or political group. For instance, a group of Jewish women and their daughters may form to look at literature written about Jews through history. African American moms and daughters may want to concentrate on African American authors. Some church groups may choose only Christian writers. In these cases, membership will be determined by likeness of the group members, and other considerations will be secondary.

If Jewish mothers wanted to form a club, they might look among people at their synagogue if they wanted to draw from an existing group, or they could post notices at other synagogues or the library to create a broader group. They would simply need to define the group and criteria for joining by making their intentions clear. For instance, a posting might say something like, "Limited to Jewish mothers and their daughters who are in fourth through sixth grades."

FIGHTING THE "EXCLUSIVE" LABEL

UNLESS YOU INVITE everyone you know to join your club, and other members invite everyone they know, there's probably no way for you to totally avoid hurt feelings from someone who would like to join your group but can't. Know that you'll have to deal with this issue sooner or later, and you'll be better prepared when it actually happens. Heather Vogel Frederick wrote about this issue in her novel *The Mother-Daughter Book Club*. The fictional club is holding its first meeting at the library, when Calliope Chadwick, a mom who wasn't asked to join the group, confronts them. Chadwick informs them that "no exclusive clubs are allowed to meet on public property." In response, Phoebe Hawthorne, one of the group's founders, says, "We're not exclusive, just private." Later, when someone suggests that maybe they should have invited Calliope and her daughter Becca, Phoebe replies, "We have every right to form a group of our own choosing. And Calliope has no right to make us feel guilty."

If you find yourself being labeled exclusive, just remember that you created a group you believe will most benefit its members and last for as long as you want it to last. If you feel pressured into including someone who isn't a good fit, you're less likely to get what you want from your club, and the group may break up sooner than you wish. If you're prepared to answer this charge, then you'll be less likely to cave in and invite someone out of guilt.

SHOULD YOU INVITE BOYS?

IT MAY SOUND silly to even bring up the question of inviting boys when we're talking about creating a mother-daughter book club, but the question may come up, particularly if other moms in your group also have sons, or if you really want to include a mom who has a son but not a daughter. Karen and I debated this issue when we were creating our club all those years ago specifically for one of these reasons: We wanted to ask a mom to join who had a son who was the same age as Madeleine and Kirsten. We ultimately decided to make our group all girls, which was all about our gut feeling that that's what was right for us.

What we couldn't anticipate was how much we would value our all-girls group years down the road. As the girls got older and we read books about female characters experiencing puberty or feeling pressured to have sex with boyfriends, the girls felt freer to say what they thought with no boys in the room. So did some of the moms. And we probably would never have planned weekends away together if there'd been a mix of girls and boys in our club.

If you invite boys, you're really creating a child-parent book club. There may be valid reasons why you want to go in that direction, but you should weigh what's most important to you.

Send Out the Invitations

You've finally decided who you want to invite, and you're ready to let other people know about the mother-daughter book club you're creating. If you know everyone on your list, the first thing you may want to do is call them up and talk to them personally about what you have in mind. Following up with a written invitation of some sort will help answer questions they may have, as well as confirm details, such as the time and place of the first meeting and the title of your first book if you have chosen it.

If you're inviting all the girls in a class and their mothers, or trying to generate interest in creating a mother-daughter

▶

▶

book club at your local library, official invitations are even more necessary. Why not have a little fun designing a piece that communicates all the details while piquing the interest of both moms and daughters? Here are some things to consider:

IF YOU KNOW EVERYONE YOU PLAN TO INVITE

- Buy party invitations and write in the details.

- Create a document on your computer with the details and print it out; then have your daughter embellish it with decorations. You can make a color copy for each person on your list.

- If you know everyone's email address, use an online invitation service, such as Evite.com or MyPunchBowl. com. The advantage is that everyone can review the list of who's invited and keep track of who is able to attend and who isn't.

IF YOU'RE CREATING A CLUB AT YOUR DAUGHTER'S SCHOOL

- Ask your daughter's teacher if it's possible to talk to the girls in the class one day.

- Create an information sheet with your contact information that the girls can take home.

- Post the sheet on a bulletin board in your daughter's classroom or in the hallway at school.

- Ask for RSVPs so you'll know how many people to expect at your informational meeting.

▶

**IF YOU'RE GENERATING INTEREST IN A CLUB
AT A LIBRARY**

- Talk to the youth librarian about reserving space on a regular basis, and ask her if she wants to be involved.

- Create an informational flyer to post on a bulletin board near the door.

- Ask if you can present to a group that meets regularly at the library, such as a teen council or a homework club.

Sample Invitation

you're invited

TO AN INFORMATIONAL MEETING
OF A NEW MOTHER-DAUGHTER BOOK CLUB

who : All fifth-grade girls and their moms

what : Monthly meetings where we discuss a book,
eat a few snacks, and have a lot of fun!

where : First meeting to be held in the school library; after that,
participants will decide on subsequent meeting place

when : MONDAY, SEPTEMBER 27, at 5:00 PM

rsvp : To Pamela, by email or phone

▶

▶

on the agenda: At this informational meeting, we'll discuss where we plan to meet, talk about a few basic ground rules, like how we'll pick the books, and spend time getting to know each other. Please come to share your ideas and enthusiasm! Snacks, juice, and water provided.

here's a list of books that may be age-appropriate for the group we're creating:

* *A YEAR DOWN YONDER,* by Richard Peck
* *BAT 6,* by Virginia Euwer Wolff
* *CADDIE WOODLAWN,* by Carol Ryrie Brink
* *DEALING WITH DRAGONS,* by Patricia Wrede
* *ELLA ENCHANTED,* by Gail Carson Levine
* *JULIE OF THE WOLVES,* by Jean Craighead George
* *OUR ONLY MAY AMELIA,* by Jennifer Holm
* *RED SCARF GIRL,* by Ji-Li Jiang
* *THE HEART OF A CHIEF,* by Joseph Bruchac
* *THE HERMIT THRUSH SINGS,* by Susan Butler

5
SETTING UP YOUR MEETINGS

" As a single mom whose other child is developmentally disabled, I find the book group is a precious time that my daughter and I share. "

—Lesly Weiner

NEW YORK, NEW YORK

SETTING THE TONE

ONCE YOU KNOW who will be in your mother-daughter book club, you can talk about other important logistics, such as how often you will meet, what day and time you'll get together, where you will gather, and how you can keep costs reasonable. When each of my clubs formed, we decided to meet over dinner at each other's homes, rotating every month on a regular schedule during the school year. We picked a night that worked best for everyone's schedule, which was the third Thursday of the month for Madeleine's club and the second Monday for Catherine's.

Where and when you get together may not be a decision you and other members have much control over. For instance, if you join a club that your local librarian is organizing, she might choose a day and time that fits into her schedule and that of other library programs. On the other hand, if you're forming your own club that happens to meet at the library, you'll have a little more flexibility. Some possible meeting places for your club include:

- Club members' homes
- Libraries
- Bookstores
- Coffee shops
- Schools
- Virtual meeting places

CHOOSING THE BEST PLACE FOR YOU

L ET'S TAKE A closer look at the options to help you decide which will work best for your group.

Club Members' Homes

PROS: If what you really want is privacy and the flexibility to decide on food and beverages you'll serve, meeting in each other's homes is your best bet. Rotating among homes gives each mom and daughter a chance to play hostess, and you can adjust meeting times more easily when scheduling conflicts arise. Outside interruptions are usually limited, so you can speak freely without worrying about non–club members overhearing.

CONS: There are issues that keep private homes from being the best meeting places for every group. Moms and daughters may be too relaxed in a home setting, and they may be tempted to hold separate conversations with the person they're sitting next to when they're lounging comfortably on a couch. If anyone in your group is allergic to pets, and others in the group have cats, dogs, hamsters, or other critters, it may not be possible to keep those homes in the rotation. It can also be a lot of work for the hostesses to tidy up their home and cook a meal for a large mother-daughter book club. This may mean that book club nights start to feel like a burden, even if you are entertaining at your house only every six months or so.

Libraries

PROS: Libraries are natural gathering places for mother-daughter book clubs. All those books neatly displayed on shelves are like a magnet for any book lover. You can enjoy wandering the stacks before and after book club meetings, and you have ready access to a youth librarian, who will probably be happy to recommend your next title. It's easy to set up, too, because you'll only need to put out a few chairs, and most libraries will allow you to bring food and drinks into their meeting rooms, so you can set snacks out on a table.

Lindsay Kahoe, who runs two mother-daughter book clubs in the Carmel Clay Public Library in Carmel, Indiana, says librarians may able to help with "book selection, conversation, and extras for your group," as well as order copies of the book you can check out.

If your library has an existing club, you can ask about joining it, or check to see if you can start a new one on your own. "The library is full of staff who are ready and eager to help people," says Kahoe. "Come prepared with ideas, but be willing to work with the library." She recommends talking with a youth or teen librarian to find out what you need to know, like whether meeting space and time are available.

CONS: Of course, you can meet only during library hours and when a meeting room isn't already reserved for a library program. Also, while most libraries will allow you to reserve and use their meeting rooms, they may require you to grant access to any community member who wants to join in. While it may be unlikely that someone you don't know will sit in when you get together, you have to be prepared for the possibility. Kahoe also says that there may be more concern over content of the books chosen, since your meetings are more likely to be public and "not every subject is right for every person."

Bookstores

PROS: Some bookstores have coffee shops that make great gathering places, and they may also have a comfortable reading area that's near the children's bookshelves where you could meet. Bookstores are great places to wander around and get ideas for your next selection either before or after you meet, and they may have knowledgeable staff that can help you choose titles. Plus, you probably need do no more than show up at a designated time and leave when you're done, so there's no work to get ready.

Kathleen March, who is children's manager at Anderson's Book Shop in Downer's Grove, Illinois, leads a mother-daughter book club there. "We created the mother-daughter book club because we want to create a community of people who read, and we want to be a meeting place for the community," says March, adding that you may find the same openness with a bookseller that you frequent.

She recommends that you check with the store manager to see if a group open to new members is already meeting. If not, ask about the possibility of starting a new club. "Even if you don't see a visible meeting space, ask the manager anyway," says March. "It may be easy to set up space where a group can come together."

Some of the things March says you should be prepared to discuss with the manager are:

- Dates and times you would like to meet
- Book selections you are considering
- Number of people who will usually attend

If you plan to have an open group, stores employees may work with you to create flyers and post meeting dates on an online schedule.

CONS: As with libraries, you'll be working your group meeting time around the bookstore's schedule, and you'll probably be out in the open where anyone passing by can overhear your discussion. The bookstore may not have a coffee shop with snacks and drinks, or if they do have a coffee shop, they may not allow food and drink outside of the seating area.

Coffee Shops

PROS: It's hard to imagine a cozier place to get together than your local coffee shop—hot cocoa with whipped cream on top for the girls, and many different hot or cold beverages for the moms to choose from. Many coffee shops have comfy, family room–like couches and overstuffed chairs to relax in, too. And all you have to do is show up at a designated time and leave when you're done. What could be easier?

CONS: On the other hand, coffee shops can be noisy, making it hard to have a group conversation that everyone can hear easily. Space may be limited, which means this venue probably works best for small mother-daughter book clubs. Finally, because you're not in a private room or a home, your conversation will be overheard by anyone who happens to be sitting around you. While that may work just fine for most books you read, when you tackle sensitive issues, the public venue may put a damper on in-depth conversation.

Schools

PROS: If all the girls in your club go to the same school, you may be able to meet after hours in the school library or in one of the classrooms. The obvious advantage is that it may be easier to set a time when everyone can meet. When the girls can just walk down the hall to the library after the bell rings at the end of the school day, it may be simple to set a time when everyone can meet. It's also easy to pack extra snacks in lunch boxes so that the girls have something to munch on while they hold a book discussion.

CONS: After school may be the most difficult time to gather if any of the moms in the group have a full-time job with inflexible hours or the girls have after-school activities.

Virtual Meeting Places

PROS: You don't have to give up on the idea of a mother-daughter book club when your members live in several different states and across more than one time zone. You can set up a group on a social networking site such as Facebook, then all gather at an agreed-upon time for a bit of virtual chatting. You can also tap into a program that uses Voice over Internet Protocol (VoIP), like Skype, which allows you to each sit at a computer and take part in a conference call. If your computer has a camera, you can even see each other while you talk.

If you don't know of other mothers and daughters willing to be in a book club, you could become part of an existing online group at sites such as GoodReads.com or LibraryThing.com, where you can join a group in progress. You and your daughter will read the books together and then comment and read what others have to say as well. It may still prompt good discussions between the two of you.

CONS: Virtual meetings don't allow you to build relationships as well as personal meetings do. The social networking sites and virtual conference calls work best for groups whose members already feel close to each other and want to stay connected. For instance, one of these options may work well for my book club with my daughter, Madeleine, who will soon be off to college. Our group has been meeting for more than eight years and we would like to find a way to continue even when the girls no longer live at home.

CHOOSING THE BEST TIME FOR YOU

DECIDING WHAT TIME and day you'll meet will depend mostly on how flexible your group members are and what other activities they're involved in. Do many of the moms in the group work full-time or odd hours? Are your girls involved in lots of after-school clubs and weekend sports? Do you reserve weekend time for whole-family events only? Once you know each mom's and daughter's restrictions, you can work around them to come up with a regular meeting time.

SET A REGULAR DATE

I CAN'T SAY ENOUGH about how important it is for you to choose a regular time for mother-daughter book club meetings. You may be working with anywhere from six to sixteen individual schedules, and if you don't have a regular meeting time each month, you're likely to reduce participation and have frustrated members. If you know that you will usually meet on the fourth Thursday of the month at 6:00 PM, it's easy to reserve that date on the calendar and turn down other invitations for the same time. Or when you always get together at 2:00 PM on the first Sunday of the month, you can plan your weekend around getting everything else done before you head to book club.

There may be occasions when you need to adjust and be flexible, like when back-to-school night is scheduled for your regular meeting time. Because things come up, you may want to look at a new date if some minimum number of mom-daughter pairs cannot attend. In my groups, we work hard to choose a date when all twelve of us can be at the meeting, but if options are limited, we settle on a date when at least eight of us can attend.

MEETINGS ON A SHOESTRING BUDGET

TWO THINGS WILL contribute to most of the expenses you incur in a mother-daughter book club: books and food. There's no reason either of these expenses needs to be excessive, and you may even find it easier than you think to get the books you need to read and provide food for a crowd on a tiny budget. Let's look at ways you can economize.

Getting the Books

It's perfectly fine if you want to buy a new copy of each book your club chooses to read. You may be one of those people who can't wait to be the first one to crack the spine of a new book and breathe the fresh ink on the page. But if you meet every month, the costs can add up. You also may want to delay buying until you know if you like the book enough to keep it in your library for repeat readings. Here's what you can do to get your hands on a copy of the book with little or no money:

- Check with your local library. If your branch doesn't have a copy, see if you can have one sent from another branch or ask for an interlibrary loan. You can usually do this online by placing a hold on the book. Our local library rarely carries the book our club will read on its shelves, but if I put a hold on the next selection as soon as I know what it will be, I usually get it with plenty of time for both my daughter and me to read it.

- Ask your librarian if she can gather several copies and hold them in the branch for you. If all your club members belong to the same library, you can ask to reserve one copy for each mother-daughter pair. Librarians will often accommodate you if there are enough copies in the system. You could also check to see if your library has book club kits. These are designed specifically for clubs with up to ten members; the kit will often contain multiple copies of the book, plus a discussion guide or other background information.

- Don't forget to look on school library shelves. Often, a school library will be more extensive than the children's or young-adult section of a public library.

- Share the book with other members of your group. If you have enough time between meetings and you know you'll be able to read the book quickly, consider sharing the cost of buying a book. One mother-daughter pair can read the book before passing it on to another. But this works only if you set a deadline for when the book has to be turned over, and then pass it along whether you're finished or not. Otherwise, it will cause too much stress for the mom and daughter who plan to have it second.

- Buy a used copy. I'm lucky enough to live in Portland, which is home to Powell's City of Books. It's an entire city block packed with new and used books, and I can usually find a reasonably priced used book in good condition. Get to know the used bookstores where you live, and if all else fails, check online for gently used books at bargain prices.

Getting your hands on a library copy or one that's used is easier if you're not reading a current bestseller. If you decide to read the latest installment of a hot series the month it's released, then everyone should expect to buy her own copy. There may be times you want to do that, but if those times are limited to once or twice a year, you should be able to keep book-buying costs down. Any money you save can go toward buying a book to be autographed when your favorite author comes to town to speak.

Cooking for a Crowd

When my first mother-daughter book club got together, it was important to us that no one get stressed over cooking for the group. Since we were gathering over dinner and discussing the books afterward, we agreed that having takeout pizza every time would be okay. But we quickly discovered that takeout pizza can be pretty hard on a budget—even if you are hosting only one of every six meetings. Plus, we got pretty tired of eating pizza every time.

Our solution was to make simple dinners that didn't strain the checkbook: Karen cooked a Crock-Pot soup and served it with rolls and salad; Yasmeen set out fixings for a taco bar; Jayne made filling for chicken pot pie in advance and froze it, adding the crust the day we met; Janelle cooked a ham she served with rolls and salad. We began eating much better and we spent less in the process. We found that with a little forethought, we could provide these delicious dinners and barely even work harder than we did when cooking only for our own families.

Even if you're not meeting for dinner, chances are your group is serving appetizers or dessert or some kind of finger foods so that everyone can munch before, during, or after book talk. Here are a few ideas that will help you to keep costs and preparation time down while eating well:

- Coordinate a potluck each time, with the hostesses providing the main dish. Assign each mom-daughter pair a dish at the preceding meeting so they'll have time to think about what they want to bring.

- Set out a dinner bar with a variety of ingredients. This works well for tacos, baked potatoes, pasta with sauces (or not), and sandwiches. Sides of carrots, chips, and fruit are easy additions. This is also a good solution if you have vegetarians in the group or if some of the daughters are picky eaters.

- If you serve appetizers, be sure to lay out lots of fresh fruit and vegetables, like carrot and celery sticks, grapes, and apples. Add a simple dip, and you've got healthy snacks that cost probably about the same as chips with dip.

- If you serve dessert instead of dinner, consider starting with the girls making dessert. Everyone can talk and catch up on the latest news while treats are in the oven, then enjoy cookies and milk with book talk.

For more simple recipes that will feed a crowd, check Appendix III, on page 271.

Coaxing a Reluctant Reader

If you're worried that your daughter won't want to be in a mother-daughter book club because she doesn't like to read, don't be discouraged. A book club can be a great place to nurture a love of reading for children of all ages, particularly if you feel that your daughter's interest in books has not been piqued. For one thing, when you get together for

▶

meetings, she'll see other moms as well as her peers talking about books they enjoyed reading. If she has fun in the social time of book club, it may encourage her to put effort into the preparation time, which involves reading the book.

Joanne Meier of Reading Rockets says that "if you have a child who is not interested in reading, it's a great opportunity to introduce all different genres of text to find out what will inspire her. Research suggests that a lot of classrooms have a wealth of stories in them, but what may be lacking is a variety of texts." She recommends offering nonfiction, poetry, and many genres of fiction in your search to spark your daughter's interest.

"We know that young kids love nonfiction," says Meier. "But you don't usually find much nonfiction in classrooms and in home libraries. It's more likely that boys are introduced to nonfiction than girls, but it turns out that girls like nonfiction as well; they just don't encounter it very much. Nonfiction provides a great opportunity to teach about real things and help kids understand their place in the world a little better."

While it may be true that your daughter can't choose every book you read in book club herself, you can talk with other members about adding more genres to your selections. From Meier's perspective, providing variety will help you hit on something your daughter loves, and her interest may snowball from there into new genres.

That certainly was the case with my daughter Catherine. When we started Catherine's book club she enjoyed reading,

▶

but she didn't like spending much time with a book. She was active and loved being outdoors, and I worried that she wouldn't want to stay in the group if she wasn't interested in the books. But we read lots of different genres in our first year: two non-fiction memoirs, one book of historical fiction, two fantasy tales, and one novel about a girl in modern times. The variety helped Catherine get much more interested in reading than she had been previously.

Of course, if you suspect your daughter has an underlying difficulty in understanding how to read, the tactics above may not help. Meier recommends you talk to her teacher about diagnosing possible learning disabilities if you see her struggling to decode words that she should be able to understand.

6
YOUR FIRST MEETING

" Having been an avid reader since I was in elementary school, I couldn't wait to share my love of reading with my own daughter. Our mother-daughter book club has been a very special way for my daughter Lily and me to enjoy books together, as well as to share thoughts, feelings, experiences, questions, and friendships. It has enriched my relationship with my daughter, and also her relationships with her friends. It is truly a treasure, and I hope that it will provide her with fond memories that will last a lifetime. "

—Jill Beres
FALLS CHURCH, VIRGINIA

READY, SET, GO!

CONGRATULATIONS! YOU'VE MADE it through setting up your club, and you're all ready to get together for the first time. Your first meeting will undoubtedly be exciting, and you'll want to make it a fun event that sets the tone for what's to come. Since you've probably never met before as a group, it's natural for you all to feel a little nervous, too. Even if the girls know each other from school and the moms are friends, it still may take time for you to get used to seeing each other at a meeting scheduled just for book club.

IT'S NOT JUST ABOUT THE BOOK

YOU MAY WANT your first get-together to be strictly social, without assigning a book to read before you gather. That way, you're free to get to know each other better and talk about a few basic book club guidelines, without feeling pressured to jump right into book discussion, too. Think about what you'd like your first meeting to accomplish, and develop a framework for what you'll do. You may want to:

- Play games that will help you all get to know each other better

- Talk about what kind of books and what genres everyone likes to read

- Plan a potluck or go out to dinner or a movie, then talk about book club plans afterward

FUN AND GAMES

PLAYING A FEW get-to-know-you games is especially important if members of your club don't know each other very well. But it's also important if you do. When you are all friends, it's easy to take for granted that you know everything there is to know about others in your group. But when you change the context of how you know each other—say, from a school group to book club or from a church group to book club—there's probably a lot you can learn. Try two or more of these games, and don't be surprised if you hear yourself say, "I didn't know that about you."

Two Truths and a Lie

Two Truths and a Lie is a classic game played by everyone from kids in day camp to adults in corporate offices. This game will have you racking your brain for wacky facts about yourself. Adults and kids alike can conjure up their dream jobs, strange foods they've tasted, unknown birthmarks, favorite music, or other little-known facts. Then you come up with a lie to rival your unusual truths. When my daughter Catherine played this game, she said, "I've eaten snails. I've eaten oxtails. I've eaten chocolate-covered crickets." Catherine's friends know she is a picky eater, so all the choices seem like a lie. But Catherine also likes to taste a lot of what she calls "weird" food. In this case, she's eaten everything but snails. When they found out the answer, everyone in the group learned something about her they didn't know before.

Introducing . . .

Mix up moms and daughters in pairs and have them interview each other. Each can spend about five minutes finding out the other's favorites: color, movie, book, food, dessert, and so on. Other questions could include: Where were you born? What is your middle name? How many houses have you lived in? What was the address of your first house? What would others be surprised to learn about you? Then you can take turns introducing each other to the rest of the group.

If I Were a Character in a Book, I Would Be . . .

Encourage everyone to give an off-the-top-of-the-head answer; that way, you're more likely to find out which character is resonating with your members at the moment. I have often wanted to be a character in a book. When I read *The Witch of Blackbird Pond,* I wanted to be Kit. When I read *Gone with the Wind,* I wanted to be Scarlett O'Hara, even though I thought of myself more as the Melanie type. At one point I even wanted to be Huckleberry Finn, floating aimlessly down the river and falling into adventures as they came. These days, I'd like to be wise like August in *The Secret Life of Bees.*

All About Me

Ask a series of questions designed to reveal both well-known and little-known facts about each of you. Here's a list to consider:

- What hobbies do you spend time doing?
- Do you now play or have you ever played a musical instrument?
- How many and what kind of pets do you have?
- If you could pick one place to travel to, where would you go?
- What would you say if you had to use three words to describe yourself?
- If you were a cartoon character, who would you be and why?
- What would you do if you could have any job you wanted?
- If you could meet any person, living or dead, who would it be and why?
- If you could eat only one thing for the rest of your life, what would it be?
- How would you spend the money if you won $1 million in the lottery?

Candy Questions

Prepare for this game by buying a candy with different colors, such as jelly beans, gumdrops, M&Ms, or Skittles. Separate the colors in advance; then have everyone take one of each. Pass around a piece of paper with color-coded questions, and ask everyone to hold up her colored candy while answering the questions from the sheet. You may be reading from something that looks like this:

- RED: What was your favorite vacation?
- BLUE: What class do you, or did you, like most in school?
- GREEN: What is your favorite ice cream flavor?
- YELLOW: Tell us something we don't know about you.
- BROWN: Name a favorite teacher.
- ORANGE: If you could change your name, what would you like it to be?

Ten Fingers

My daughter Madeleine loves this game, and she plays it with her friends frequently. Everyone sits in a circle, holding up both hands and all ten fingers. One person starts by saying something she has not done. Anyone who has done it has to clap and put a finger down. For instance, you might say, "I have never ridden a horse." Anyone who has ridden a horse then claps and puts a finger down, and anyone who hasn't continues to hold all ten fingers up. Go around the circle and have each person say something she hasn't done.

The game can end in one of two ways: You can play until one person has no fingers left showing, or you can play until only one person has any fingers showing. You will want to choose something that you know most other people in the group have done and you haven't, since the goal is to be the last one with fingers showing. Madeleine says movies you've never seen, food you've never eaten, and places you've never been are good categories. For instance, if you think most people have been to Disneyland and you haven't, it would be strategic for you to say, "I've never been to Disneyland."

"Everyone is always surprised when I say I've never eaten cheesecake," says Madeleine. "Ten Fingers is so much fun, we never want to stop once we start playing."

STARTING WITH A BOOK

YOU MAY BE so excited to start reading together that you can't resist beginning with a book assignment. You can still work one or two get-to-know-you games into the mix if this is the case, and you'll just have less time to be social during your first meeting.

It's best to begin your first meeting with a social activity. Doing so ensures that even latecomers have arrived by the time you're ready to talk about the book. At the first meeting, you can enjoy snacks or a meal while you chat, play a game or two, then gather around for book discussion. Before you dive into the book you've just read, you may want to spend a few minutes talking about basic expectations for your group, and let everyone talk about why she wanted to be part of it. You can also ask what particular literary genre each person likes. This doesn't mean you'll be limited to the genres favored by the majority;

it's more a way of learning the types of books that each member may tend to recommend.

You will want to know which mom-daughter pair is on tap to pick your next selection, so both of them can be prepared to give a short synopsis of what the following month's book pick is about.

START WITH A SPLASH

ANOTHER WAY TO hold your first meeting is to make it a celebration. You can all meet at a restaurant, spend most of your time together socializing and getting to know each other, and then talk about book club. Or you can go out to a movie together, then meet for a book club chat over ice cream. You could even start with a big event, like Gina's book club of moms and fifth-grade girls—called the Book Chicks—did in St. Peters, Missouri. Here's their story, told by Gina.

"I picked up Heather Vogel Frederick's book *The Mother-Daughter Book Club* quite by accident this past summer and read it while my daughter had swimming lessons. I was so impressed with the book and the concept of a book club group for moms and daughters that I decided to research the whole idea and began our own little book club.

"On a whim, I emailed Heather to see if she might be able to speak to our group of girls, and I found out she was already planning to be in the St. Louis area during the exact week that we planned our book club discussion meeting. She was so gracious and offered to come visit our very first book club meeting in person! Our group was completely over the moon to have the author of the very first book we've read as a group, and of the very book that inspired the club's beginning in the first place, come and talk with our girls and to share her love of the written word and her story."

As you can imagine, everyone in Gina's group left her first meeting excited about being in a new book club together. Even though few clubs will be able to schedule an author to join them when they're just starting out, the idea is to plan an event that will leave everyone looking forward to the next get-together.

Sample Ground Rules

You may think that asking everyone in your new group to agree to a set of ground rules sounds too formal and unnecessary. After all, why would you need to set ground rules when everyone is excited about being part of your new mother-daughter book club? Ground rules serve two main purposes:

- They make sure that moms and daughters know what is expected of them when they agree to be part of the club.

- If a conflict arises between members down the road, these rules can be a handy reference for solving any disputes.

Ground rules don't need to be hard and fast laws that no one is allowed to break, but rather just be a few simple guidelines that make sense for your group. Don't assume that because something seems intuitive to you, everyone

▶

else will feel the same way. For instance, you'll want to make sure that the mothers and daughters in your group expect to come to most meetings as a pair. You don't want meetings to routinely become a place for a harried mom to drop off her daughter for a couple of hours, and you don't routinely want a mom who shows up alone while her daughter is at sports practice.

The key word in these scenarios is "routinely." Everyone has a busy life, and something may come up occasionally for anyone in the group. You really do want a mom or daughter to attend without the other if this happens infrequently. But if one of your members makes a habit of this, it shows that she's not truly committed to your book club. It's best to get this expectation out in the open at the beginning.

Another issue you may want to cover in your ground rules is the expectation that everyone read the book. Again, this may not be a concern at the beginning, but it is more difficult to have a meaningful discussion if many of your members haven't read the book. As schedules and commitments change down the road, you want to be sure that everyone expects to prioritize reading for book club.

You may also want to consider setting up expectations for participating in group discussions, including respecting others' opinions even if you disagree. A good set of ground rules won't feel oppressive or overbearing but should help make sure that those in your group place a certain amount of importance on the club you're starting.

▶

Here's a sample list that you can use as-is or adapt to your specific group:

MOTHER-DAUGHTER BOOK CLUB GROUND RULES

As a member of the [insert name here] Mother-Daughter Book Club, I agree that:

- I will try my best to read each book we select, even if it's not the type of book I usually read.

- I will do my best to attend each meeting with my mom/daughter.

- I will participate in discussions.

- I will listen attentively when others in the group are talking.

- I will be respectful when I disagree with others' opinions.

7
CHOOSING THE BOOKS

> " Our mother-daughter book club experience has been extremely positive. It's an activity we can both participate in. We love to read books and to join the discussions. It's laugh-out-loud fun!"
>
> —Lisa Newman
> BETHEL PARK, PENNSYLVANIA

EENY, MEENY, MINY, MOE

ALTHOUGH I ALWAYS have a stack of books on my bedside table waiting for me to read, I can still be stumped when it comes time to choose something for my book clubs. I talk about possibilities in advance with Madeleine and Catherine so we can decide together, but making the "best choice for the group" seems to add extra pressure. We're reluctant to recommend a book we know someone else in the group will probably not like, and if we haven't read it already, we don't even know if we'll like it ourselves. I think deep-down most of us want to pick the book that everyone in book club loves, the book that gives us a lot to think about and talk about, the book that will linger in our memories for years to come as one of the best selections ever. That's a pretty tall order.

DIALING BACK THE PRESSURE

CHOOSING THE BOOKS your group will read doesn't have to be stressful, particularly if you keep in mind that in all likelihood, no one else in your group expects you to pick the perfect book. I find that most mother-daughter book club members are looking for a book that:

- Holds their interest while they read
- Appeals to both girls and their moms
- Provokes a good discussion during the meeting

You may think that still seems like a tall order. Fortunately, there are many great books you can read that fit these criteria. Later in this chapter, you'll learn more about how to find them.

MOMS VS. DAUGHTERS—WHO GETS TO PICK?

YOU MIGHT BE tempted to forget that your group is a mother-daughter book club. By that I mean you may let girls make all the decisions when picking the books, or you may think that only moms are able to choose what's best. Either of these perceptions can create problems. If daughters choose the books each time, you run the risk that they will often opt for pop-culture books that are fun to read but present little to discuss. If moms choose each time, you may end up with a string of books meant to teach a lesson that the girls aren't ready to learn.

I advocate for involving both generations in the decision, and here are a couple of reasons why:

- Both moms and daughters will read the book, so it should be something they can both enjoy.

- Moms and daughters both benefit when they talk about what will make a good selection and why.

GROUP OR INDIVIDUAL CHOICE?

YOU'LL ALSO NEED to think about whether you prefer to choose your selections by group vote or to rotate the choice among members. Both of my book groups leave the choice up to the mom and daughter who will host the next meeting. In most cases, whoever is hosting next comes prepared with a book to recommend. But sometimes they can't decide and bring several books to choose from. In that case, everyone gets a say in which one we read.

Either of these methods also works if you pick out books for more than one meeting at a time. You can ask everyone to bring a single book to recommend, then decide when you'll read each one. Or everyone can bring several books and you can pick the ones getting the most votes, regardless of who brought them.

Why would you want to choose several books and assign them ahead of time? When you know what you'll be reading a few months or even a year in advance, you can dive right in at any time, instead of waiting for a new assignment after each meeting. If everyone has a busy schedule, this approach can make it easier for moms and daughters to finish reading the book in time. The downside is that you lose flexibility, so if a new book comes out that everyone would really like to read, you may have to wait and add it to your list months later.

Another option is to choose a longer book and read it a little bit at a time over several months or more. That's the format Heather Vogel Frederick chose for her characters when she wrote *The Mother-Daughter Book Club.* The fictional group tackled *Little Women,* a classic that would be difficult to assign as a selection for a single meeting. By reading the book in sections, the club got to discuss each part in detail. In her second book, *Much Ado About Anne,* Frederick has club members reading *Anne of Green Gables.*

Other lengthy possibilities include *Gone with the Wind, David Copperfield, Treasure Island,* and *Harry Potter.* The challenge with reading one book over a longer period of time is knowing when to stop. It will certainly be tempting to read ahead once you've completed the assigned number of pages for any month.

FINDING GOOD BOOKS

I LIKE SEARCHING FOR good books almost as much as I like reading them. I can lose track of time wandering the aisles of a bookstore or perusing shelves in the library. For me, bringing a new find home and opening the cover for the first time is like unwrapping a present, and I never get tired of it. Even though there's more pressure involved in choosing a book for my reading groups, it's still a lot of fun. My daughters and I will go back and forth over the pros and cons of our possible picks until we settle on a recommendation. Often we really want to read the titles we reject, too, so we'll put those aside to read on our own.

We rarely read the books before we choose them for our group, and that's true of most of the other moms and daughters in our clubs. We like discovering new titles together, even if that means we don't always like what we read. You may want to talk with members of your book club and decide if you can choose books that are new to you or if you want to restrict book choices to ones you have read already.

Here is a list of possible sources to help you find books for your club.

Friends

Ask your friends what they're reading, especially if you know their tastes are similar to yours. Get them to describe the story for you, and watch how animated they are as they talk. It may give you a clue about what you can expect during discussion with your group.

Librarians

A school librarian may be particularly helpful if she knows some or all of the girls in your group. You can also cultivate a relationship with the youth librarian at the local branch of your town's public library. Talk to her about books that have been most successful with your group in the past, and ask her to suggest others that will give you lots to talk about.

Bookstore Employees

People who work at bookstores usually read a lot, too, and I find that they're often more than willing to share a list of titles they're excited about. You may even find short summaries of employee recommendations taped to the shelves where the books are displayed, making it easy to target staff favorites.

Online Resources

Book-related websites can also provide good suggestions. My site, www.motherdaughterbookclub.com, offers the advantage of listing books by age group that have been recommended by other mother-daughter book clubs. Other reliable sources include:

- School Library Journal: www.schoollibraryjournal.com
- KidsReads.com: www.kidsreads.com
- TeenReads.com: www.teenreads.com
- Newbery Medal Winners: www.ala.org/ala/mgrps/divs/alsc/ awardsgrants/bookmedia/newberymedal/newberymedal.cfm
- Young Reader's Choice Awards: www.pnla.org/yrca/index.htm

CHOOSING BOOKS FOR AN AGE RANGE

IF YOUR GIRLS are not all the same age, you'll need to spend a little more time making sure your choice will work for everyone. If you pick something that's too challenging for or not relevant to your younger members, they may become frustrated and give up. Conversely, if your older members find your selections too easy and the issues not mature enough, they may lose interest. You can often ask for a recommended age range when you're talking to a librarian or someone in a bookstore. Websites may list an appropriate age alongside book reviews.

SHOULD YOU READ BOOKS ASSIGNED IN SCHOOL?

THIS IS A question that's bound to come up in your group sooner or later, so you may as well tackle it now. There are two schools of thought on whether books assigned for literature classes at school are good selections for a mother-daughter book club.

On the one hand, if you know that girls are assigned to read a book and there's little time for them to read anything else, reading school assignments may be a practical way for your group to keep going even if time is tight. Your discussions may also benefit, because if the girls are discussing a book in class, they are likely to have insights to share that you wouldn't otherwise have.

On the other hand, if you're reading the same things the girls read in school, book club can start to feel like just another assignment. You want it to be something they look forward to each month, not extra homework.

Personally, I prefer keeping book club selections and schoolwork separate when at all possible. I believe the value of reading just for the pleasure of it is an important lifetime habit to instill, and book club is one of the best places to accomplish that.

Books To Get You Started

Here's a list of ten books in four age groups recommended by mother-daughter book clubs around the country to help you get started. These favorites fit the criteria listed earlier that define a good book club pick: They hold your interest while you read, they appeal to both girls and their moms, and they provoke good discussions during your meeting. For a synopsis of each title, see the listings in Appendix II, at the back of the book.

AGES SEVEN AND EIGHT

It's always important to make sure some of what you're reading is fun, but it's especially important at this age. This is the time when you're really setting the stage for your daughters to develop a lifelong love of literature. While many of the works may be challenging for your daughters to read on their own, reading out loud to them will give you a good opportunity to talk about the story and what you are learning from it as you go along. Then, when you meet with your group on book club night, you'll both already have ideas of what you want to talk about.

- *Bed-Knob and Broomstick,* by Mary Norton

- *Charlie and the Chocolate Factory,* by Roald Dahl

- *Charlotte's Web,* by E. B. White

- *The Hundred Dresses,* by Eleanor Estes

- *The Mouse and the Motorcycle,* by Beverly Cleary

- *Pippi Longstocking,* by Astrid Lindgren

- *Sarah, Plain and Tall,* by Patricia MacLachlan

▶

- *The Secret School,* by Avi

- *Tales of a Fourth-Grade Nothing,* by Judy Blume

- *The Year of the Dog,* by Grace Lin

AGES NINE AND TEN

While you may still choose to read out loud to your daughters at this age, they are more likely to be able to read on their own and appreciate books with more complicated issues. Choosing a memoir for your group, like *Boy,* by Roald Dahl, or *Red Scarf Girl,* by Ji-Li Jiang, will help your daughters begin to see reading as an interesting way to learn more about real people, as well as fictional characters.

- *Bat 6,* by Virginia Euwer Wolff

- *11 Birthdays,* by Wendy Maas

- *Boy,* by Roald Dahl

- *Caddie Woodlawn,* by Carol Ryrie Brink

- *Granny Torrelli Makes Soup,* by Sharon Creech

- *The Hermit Thrush Sings,* by Susan Butler

- *Julie of the Wolves,* by Jean Craighead George

- *The Mother-Daughter Book Club,* by Heather Vogel Frederick

- *Our Only May Amelia,* by Jennifer Holm

- *Red Scarf Girl,* by Ji-Li Jiang

AGES ELEVEN TO THIRTEEN

Just like your girls, the subject matter of books you read may start to mature at this stage. Plots are more complicated, characters are more likely to be put in situations the girls may face in real life, and you may read about characters engaging in risky social behavior. Keep in mind that your daughters need to know your own values, and reading books on touchy subjects provides a safe setting in which you and your daughter can discuss issues that make you uncomfortable.

- *A Year Down Yonder,* by Richard Peck
- *Al Capone Does My Shirts,* by Gennifer Choldenko
- *Angus, Thongs and Full-Frontal Snogging,* by Louise Rennison
- *Bloomability,* by Sharon Creech
- *Everything on a Waffle,* by Polly Horvath
- *Flipped,* by Wendelin Van Draanen
- *Framed,* by Frank Cottrell Boyce
- *Hattie Big Sky,* by Kirby Larson
- *The House of the Scorpion,* by Nancy Farmer
- *Tangerine,* by Edward Bloor
- *Zlata's Diary,* by Zlata Filipovic

AGES FOURTEEN AND UP

When your daughters are in high school, you may decide to start choosing books from the adult category, as well as

▶

from the young-adult list. This is also an important time to choose books that are both fun to read and meaningful. Often, the books assigned to teens in literature classes at school can be what Madeleine and Catherine call "depressing and tedious," because they're meant to teach a lesson. To make sure reading doesn't seem like another assignment or a chore, check the reading list for your school and choose different books.

- *A Northern Light,* by Jennifer Donnelly
- *The Absolutely True Diary of a Part-time Indian,* by Sherman Alexie
- *An Abundance of Katherines,* by John Green
- *The Book Thief,* by Markus Zusak
- *Light Years,* by Tammar Stein
- *North of Beautiful,* by Justina Chen Headley
- *Pride and Prejudice,* by Jane Austen
- *The Secret Life of Bees,* by Sue Monk Kidd
- *Speak,* by Laurie Halse Anderson
- *West with the Night,* by Beryl Markham

8
WHAT WILL YOU DO AT MEETINGS?

" My favorite part of being in our mother-daughter book club is having the opportunity to observe and share in my daughter's interactions with her peers. I feel like I have been given a gift of insight and perspective into what is really important and relevant in the girls' lives. "

—Marci Rosenthal
CANTON, MASSACHUSETTS

ENGAGING BOTH MOMS AND DAUGHTERS

YEARS AGO, WHEN I was in a women's book club with friends in the area, we met once a month, drank wine, ate snacks, and spent a little time socializing before talking about the book we read. This may be the model you have in mind for the group you create with your daughter, and it may work just fine for you. But mother-daughter book clubs involve adults *and* children. That means you may need to give a little more thought to incorporating other activities, like games or crafts, when you get together for meetings.

START WITH SOCIAL TIME

WHEN MY DAUGHTERS were younger, they would greet girls as they arrived at our home for book club, then run upstairs with their friends to their bedroom. The door would shut, and the moms downstairs could hear bumps, thuds, and laughter. As long as no one was crying, we figured they were all okay. While the girls were closeted away upstairs, we moms sipped on wine or soft drinks and caught up on what had been happening with each other during the last month. Any stress over worries at work or home quickly melted away as we immersed ourselves in conversation.

As the girls got older, the upstairs activity got calmer, but it served the same purpose. It gave both moms and daughters separate time to reconnect and relax before we started to discuss the book. Even now, with our daughters in high school, we still begin each meeting that way.

Starting your meetings with a social activity is important if you want to have meaningful discussions later. That's because most of us need time to warm up when we get together with a group, even if it is a group of friends. How you choose to spend that social time depends on your individual club. You may want to leave the time unstructured, like we do, and reconnect over conversation alone. You may also decide to work together on a craft, cook dessert, or play a game. As long as what you decide fits your group and its members, it will be the right choice for you.

Denise's club members enjoy playing games, so they've played many over the years they have been meeting. One of their favorites is to ask moms and daughters to compare their favorite things at a specific age: They have talked about favorite books, holidays, birthdays, crushes, schoolteachers, movies, plays, and more. Each person who names a favorite also has to say why it was her favorite at the time. Denise says that some of these conversations, especially the ones about clothes, were hilarious.

Creative members in Denise's club have also designed board games specifically for a book they were discussing. "We had a tailor-made Trivial Pursuit for *The Little Princess,* and a tailor-made Sorry for *The Downsiders,*" says Denise. "With *The Gospel According to Larry,* a story about consumerism, we had a competition to see how many trademarks each of us knew. We all knew a scary number."

Denise says she likes playing games in her book club because they are a fun way to help everyone get to know each other better.

Sheila's club likes to start with an art project, an activity that allows them all to quietly reconnect before they start talking. Such projects have included beading, drawing, and painting. "Some of the girls see each other more often than others, so when we get together they want to talk about the things they've been doing," says Sheila. "The art project helps to get them all together because it is something they can all get involved in right away."

PROGRESS TO A SNACK OR A MEAL

ONCE YOU'VE RECONNECTED socially, you can move on to serving food. Even if you're meeting at a library or a bookstore, chances are you'll serve finger foods, such as veg-etables and fruit with juice or water, or other little bites to snack on. If you're serving a full meal at someone's home, consider creating separate eating spaces for moms and daughters. This is especially important if you started off with everyone mak-ing crafts or playing games together. Girls and moms will both appreciate time to talk to their peers without worrying about what the other generation overhears.

You may also consider ways to tie your snacks or meal into the theme of the book. When we read *Everything on a Waffle,* by Polly Horvath, with Madeleine's book club, we met at Yasmeen and Sophie's house. Yasmeen made waffles for dinner, a novelty that was a hit with all of us. Even years later, Madeleine remem-bers that night as "a really creative way to tie our dinner to the theme of the book."

We've had quite a few themed dinners since then, and I have found that matching food to a theme in the book helps to set the tone for an evening of fun. Many books lend themselves to cooking themed dinners to match. While you may not see a con-nection to something as creative as putting chicken pot pie on a waffle, you will often find many references to food in a book. When Catherine and I read *The Secret Life of Bees* in book club, we weren't surprised to find honey on the menu at Ellen's house that night. She also cooked good Southern favorites mentioned in the book, like corn fritters and green beans. Just dishing up got us all ready to talk about what we had read.

GATHER TO TALK ABOUT THE BOOK

IF YOUR GROUP is like many other mother-daughter book clubs, you'll have so much fun socializing and eating, you may forget that it's really important to leave plenty of time to talk about the book. While your prediscussion activities can build friendships and encourage bonding between mothers and daughters in your group, having an in-depth exchange about the book will help you get to know one another even more intimately. When you leave adequate time for this part of your book club meetings, you make sure that members who need to leave soon after you begin won't disrupt the flow of conversation.

Ideas to help you make the most of your time talking about the book can be found in the next chapter, but here are a couple of things for you to think about before you begin: Keep in mind that any time you transition from one activity to another, you will need a few moments to settle down. Physically moving from one place to another—like from the dining table to the couch— clues everyone in that it's time to finish individual conversations and get ready for group discussion.

Another way to help the transition time is to ask a simple question that everyone can answer at the same time. For instance, you can ask moms and daughters to give the book a star rating from one to five, with five being the highest, or ask them to give it a grade of A to F. Emma's club starts by asking everyone to give a thumbs-up or a thumbs-down, and each mom and daughter says a few words about why she voted one way or the other. Sheila's club always starts with an ice-breaker question. For instance, when they read *Hattie Big Sky,* by Kirby Larson, the question was "If you were going to be a farm animal, what would you be?" You can also ask whoever chose the book to say why she recommended it. Simple questions like these will focus everyone's attention and help you get started.

LEAVE THEM WANTING MORE

SOMETIMES BOOK TALK can go on until you begin to come back to some of the same issues you've already covered. This is probably a clue that you can wrap up. An easy way to signal that the meeting is ending is to bring up your next meeting. You can say something like, "I believe Margaret and Theresa are hosting next time; can you tell us about the book you've picked, and then we'll look at dates?" After that, everyone can gather up her things and head out the door until the next book club meeting.

FEEL FREE TO MIX IT UP

CARRIE'S BOOK CLUB schedules time for crafts, food, and book talk, but not in the order discussed above. Her group starts with something to eat, moves on to talking about what they read, then finishes with a craft. At each meeting the girls spend about thirty minutes making a bookmark. It's a simple activity that's easy to prepare for in advance, and it lets the meeting finish with social time. Carrie says, "It's really worked out well for our group. The girls are having fun discovering new books and creating fun commemorative bookmarks."

Emma's group also surrounds discussion time with socializing, but in a different way from Carrie's. Emma says her group spends time "chatting at arrival to warm up and let everyone get comfortable; then we start discussing the book, and we talk about the next book and meeting date. Lastly, we have dessert and socialize some more."

As you can see, the guidelines above are meant to be just that—guidelines that help you decide what will work for your group.

Make Time for Moms Only

A few years after Catherine and I started our book club, one of the moms in the group, Ellen, suggested that the mothers get together without their daughters for a holiday celebration. My immediate thought was to say yes. Then feelings of guilt set in. *We can't meet without our daughters; they'll think we want time away from them,* I thought. *They'll think we don't love them.* Fortunately, others in the group were not so burdened, because many of the moms spoke up to say, "What a great idea. When should we do it?"

We picked a date and decided to meet at Ellen's house to watch the movie *Love Actually* and eat dessert. The night of the event, I set off by myself with a plate of cookies to share, and tried to push lingering guilt aside. As soon as I joined the group, my doubts vanished. Everyone was having such a good time, I knew this was a good idea. We sipped dessert wine while we snacked on treats and talked for a while, before heading upstairs to the TV room. We settled in comfortably, turned the movie on, then spent the next two

▶

▶

hours alternately laughing and crying. When it was all over, we went home thoroughly happy, vowing to do it again the next year.

You may be like me, thinking that arranging an event for just the moms is a little selfish. After all, without the daughters, your group would be just another book club, right? But I'll bet you also think nothing of having your daughter get together with her book club friends on her own, without you. There may even be times when all the book club daughters go out to see a school play or have ice cream. I doubt you think of them as being selfish.

The fact is, it's often much easier for moms to see benefits when their children socialize with peers than it is for them to recognize that those same benefits apply to adults as well. We act differently when we're around peers than when we're in mixed child-adult groups. We become less like teachers, and more like children at play. We may talk more freely, without worrying about the need to censor our words for young audiences. We may also gain insights into each other's lives that would never surface if we didn't have mom-only time.

The idea is to create time for yourselves. You can go out to dinner, stay in and watch a movie, go bowling, or even go on a hike together. Whatever you do, you'll want to create an environment where you can talk freely and have fun. No guilt allowed.

9
MANAGING YOUR DISCUSSIONS

" I love the leadership that each girl brings to our book group—whether it's their thoughtful questions and insights or being in charge of the snack or craft. It's a fun way to get to know all the girls better—including my own. **"**

—Carrie Chute
BELLINGHAM, WASHINGTON

WHY PLAN YOUR DISCUSSION?

WHEN YOU THINK about all the fun opportunities for reading and socializing that mother-daughter book clubs have to offer, it's easy to forget that having meaningful discussions is an important part of book club, too.

Why can't you just open with a simple question like "What did everyone think of the book?" Here's what can happen when you plan your discussion that way:

- You may struggle to get girls and moms to say more than "I liked it" or "I hated it."

- Everyone will have a lot to say, but you'll jump around from topic to topic and miss out on thoughtful dialogue.

- With no specific focus, your talk can go off on any number of tangents that have nothing to do with the book you read.

While it shouldn't take you hours to prepare, spending a few moments to create a plan for your book discussion will help everyone get the most out of your talk. Here's what you can do to ease the process along.

CHOOSE A LEADER

ONE OF THE first things you need to decide is who will lead your discussion. When everyone knows who's in charge, your group is more likely to stay on track.

Who should lead the discussion? An easy way to decide is to say that whoever chooses the book should come up with discussion questions. This makes sense because if you've chosen the book, it probably contains ideas you thought would be interesting to talk about. But if the mom-daughter pair who chose the book are also hosting, you may not want to add another task to their prep list.

A mother-daughter book club with eight moms and eight girls in Brookfield, Wisconsin, found a way to spread the meeting preparation time around. "To make it fun for everyone, each of our meetings is hosted by one mother-daughter pair, and the discussion is led by another pair," says Julie, one of the moms in the group. Julie says this works well for her group because no one has to spend too much time getting ready for their meetings.

PREPARE IN ADVANCE

HERE'S A LIST of things you can do to help prepare for your meeting—don't forget to include your daughter in the prep work. When you research a book or develop questions together, you let your daughter know you value her input. You may also be surprised by the questions she raises. And if your work together leads to a conversation between just the two of you, that's part of what mother-daughter book club is all about!

- Take notes while you're reading. Use a blank piece of paper to note the page numbers containing special passages that mean something to you, or mark the pages with sticky notes. That way, it will be easy to turn to a page in the book to illustrate your point or someone else's when the discussion is in full swing.

- Look for resources online. Can you find a discussion guide for the book you read? Does the author have a website where she talks about her book? Is there important historical information you can find that may help you understand the time period or place where the book is set? Can you find a blog so you can see what others are saying online about the topics covered in the book?

- Talk to a librarian. Go to or call your local library and find out if the youth librarian has read the book you'll be discussing. If she has, she may be able to recommend a list of discussion questions. You can also check with your school's librarian for ideas about discussion topics. If she knows all or most of the girls in your group, she may be able to come up with questions that will resonate particularly well with them.

- Develop a list of eight to ten questions, but remember to be flexible. Groups are dynamic, which means you can't always anticipate exactly how a conversation will evolve. If the topic moves off your predetermined list of questions, feel free to go with the flow, as long as the new direction is relevant to what you've read.

CREATE THE ENVIRONMENT

GATHER COMFORTABLY AND sit where everyone can see all the others in your group. If you're meeting at a home, consider having people sit on throw pillows on the floor if there's not enough room for everyone to get cozy on couches. If you're meeting at a library or bookstore, sit at a round table if possible. Making eye contact is important while you're talking. Turn down any loud music or other distractions.

DURING THE DISCUSSION

KEEP THESE POINTS in mind while you're leading the discussion:

- Start and end on time. Club members have set aside time to be at the meeting. But daughters probably have other obligations, like sports, homework, and family activities, while moms may have taken off from work early to be available. By getting started at an agreed-upon time, you let everyone know that discussions are an important part of your meetings, and people don't have to feel rushed when talking about the book. When you end on time, you show respect for the commitment everyone makes to the group.

- Ask "why" questions. These tend to get past the obvious narrative elements and reveal more about the personal responses to the book and the personalities of the group members themselves. For instance, if a girl or a mom answers a question about *why* she believes Opal loved Winn-Dixie so much, she will probably have a lot more to say than she would if she were asked simply, "Do you believe Opal loved Winn-Dixie?"

- Give everyone enough time to talk. Whether you go around in a circle or have club members comment randomly, listen to people's answers before rushing on to the next person or weighing in with your own opinions. Remember that you're leading an open discussion, not pushing an agenda.

- Ask questions that both girls and moms will want to answer. For instance, moms and daughters can both talk about how they think our society perceives physical beauty during a discussion on *Uglies,* by Scott Westerfeld. A question to encourage perspectives from both generations could be "How do you see physical beauty being promoted in our world?"

- Don't preach. Girls know when moms are more interested in getting a message across than in having a genuine discussion about something they've read. For instance, when talking about the main character in *Speak,* a teenage girl named Melinda who is raped at a party she attends before starting high school, a mom may be tempted to give a sermon about the dangers of parties. She can shut down the conversation entirely by making a statement like, "Melinda would have never been raped if she hadn't been at that party in the first place. I hope you've learned something from reading about what happened to her." A more effective way of getting daughters to open up and draw out conversation is to ask instead, "What do you think Melinda could have done differently to protect herself at the party?"

- Avoid asking leading questions. A leading question suggests that you're expecting to get a specific answer. If you ask, "I can't believe any driver's ed teacher would act the way Mr. Fielding does in *Driver's Ed,* can you?" you're not likely to encourage much further discussion. This kind of question assumes that everyone in the group believes what you do, and others may be uncomfortable saying, "I disagree." Instead, ask a question like, "How believable do you think Mr. Fielding is as a driver's ed teacher?"

- Gently seek out someone who hasn't joined in the conversation yet. You can say, "We haven't heard what Rachael has to say on the subject yet. Rachael, why do you think the goose girl wanted to keep her true identity a secret?" This may draw out the quieter members of your group without shining the spotlight in their eyes.

- Don't embarrass anyone by dismissing her opinion. If you say, "I can't believe you think it was a good idea for Dinnie [in *Bloomability*] to go to boarding school in Switzerland; I think it was a dumb idea," you'll probably end the conversation and make others in the group reluctant to speak out. If you find someone's answer to a question surprising, ask her to elaborate by saying, "I'd like to know more about why you feel that way."

- Keep the conversation relevant to the book. Because book club meetings are so social, it's inevitable that someone's comment will remind a mom or daughter about a similar experience in her life, and that memory will make someone else think about something else entirely. If you're talking about *A Year Down Yonder* and Grandma Dowdel's scheme to outwit the boys who plan to tip over her outhouse on Halloween night, it could be easy for someone to tell a story about the time her grandma chased a mouse from her kitchen into her bedroom. Gently bring the conversation back on track by saying something like, "I think we all have stories to tell about our grandmas—maybe we can do that if we have time at the end of our book discussion. What else did Grandma Dowdel do that surprised you?"

- Wrap up with the same question every time. This can be a good signal to the group that discussion is ending and it's time to talk about the details of your next meeting. You could ask everyone to rate the book on a scale of one to ten, or assign it a grade from A to F. Or you could ask each person to say if she would recommend the book to someone else, and why or why not.

SHOULD EVERYONE BE REQUIRED TO TALK?

AFTER YOUR GROUP has been meeting for a few months, you'll likely discover a pattern in your discussions similar to one that emerged in one of my mother-daughter book clubs. Each time our group gathered, everyone would happily chat away over dinner and dessert until one of the moms noticed the time and rounded us all up for book discussion. We'd sit in a circle and begin to talk about what we had read. Discussion was always lively and flowed along quite naturally, but there was only one problem: We didn't hear from everyone, because some girls never talked at all, and some of the moms didn't say much either. Most of the comments came from the same moms and daughters every time.

What should you do if you encounter this problem? First, you need to decide how important it is for your club to encourage everyone to participate. We talked about the pros and cons of each approach to help us decide. On the one hand, we talked about all the negatives of requiring everyone to participate in discussions. On the other, we ticked off the benefits of having more of us talk about the book. Our list of reasons why requiring everyone to talk wouldn't work included these points:

- Some moms and daughters are just not comfortable expressing their opinions in a group. If they are pushed too hard to participate, they may not enjoy coming to meetings anymore.

- It can be embarrassing to be put on the spot and have to come up with something to say even when you can't think of anything.

- If you say that everyone must talk, and then some in the group still don't, you won't want to enforce the rule.

Our list of reasons why requiring everyone to talk is a good thing included these points:

- Hearing a broader range of perspectives from a greater number of people can help everyone learn something about the themes or characters in a book. You may not like the book you've read for book club, but hearing others speak about what they liked or found interesting can help you appreciate it better.

- Speakers get to practice expressing their thoughts verbally in a safe setting. It is easy to see how this benefits the girls, who may be required to give speeches in school regularly. But even moms can benefit from learning to speak up and say what's on their minds. It could help with everything from participating in meetings at work to making a point to talking to a mechanic fixing their car.

- When you hear people express their thoughts about issues in a book, you get to know them better. There is no easier way to build strong, close relationships with everyone in your group.

Our group decided the pros of having everyone speak up outweighed the cons of continuing as we were. Our solution was to say that for each discussion, the mom and daughter who had chosen the book would develop two or three questions that everyone would answer. Then we'd branch out into more questions and make participation optional.

We saw great results at our very next meeting. With gentle prompting, even the shiest among us had something to say and seemed to be comfortable saying it. Our discussions became richer as a result.

If your club plans to get everyone talking during meetings, keep a few things in mind. First, let everyone know there will be a change, and talk about why you think it's important. Expect there to still be times when some of you don't have much to say. That's okay. Remember, the purpose of requiring people to speak up isn't to force everyone to talk; it's more to create a forum where you can all feel comfortable sharing your views.

WHAT CAN YOU DO WHEN SOMEONE TALKS TOO MUCH?

WHAT IF YOUR group is experiencing just the opposite problem? What if one or more members of your group dominate the conversation and make it difficult to hear what everyone else wants to say? This can be tricky to address, because you want to be respectful to the speaker while also limiting her time at the podium.

Katie O'Dell is the school-age services manager for the Multnomah County Library in Portland, Oregon, where she oversees a summer-reading program for more than fifty-eight thousand youths, and book discussion groups systemwide. Throughout much of her career, O'Dell has led children's book clubs, and she offers the following advice for dealing with a nonstop talker.

"There are several reasons why people participating might dominate the discussion, but ultimately some basic ground rules and occasional built-in reminders at each meeting can relieve this. Members who talk a lot might be nervous and not self-aware of how much they are sharing. They may be passionate about the topic and wanting to share with the group. They may want to be acting as a role model for their own child to talk and just not noticing the nonverbal cues from others in the group to include more people. They may have little experience in a book discussion group and not understand the unspoken ground rules.

"Sometimes people talk a lot because they're excited about the topic being discussed, and they want to make sure they say everything they're thinking. They may be nervous speaking in a group, or lose track of the point they're trying to make and ramble on a bit. It's easy for any of us to be in this position at some time, but it's best if someone can keep the group on track by interrupting nicely and moving the conversation to someone else."

O'Dell says she finds that moms who dominate discussions are "often either nervous and compensating for that by speaking too much or are more interested in being at the group than their child is. When young people dominate discussion, it's often because they haven't learned others' nonverbal clues about when to end and invite others to speak, or they are so excited and energized by the book, they have trouble controlling their impulses." She recommends addressing "dominating book group members quickly and with grace to ensure their continued participation while helping to shape their contribution to match group expectations." O'Dell offers the following helpful tips:

- "One easy trick that I use frequently as a facilitator is turning my body to be open to the entire group and saying, 'I'd like to hear what someone else has to say on that topic.'"

- "Another good lead is 'I've got a good picture of your opinion on this book; what do the rest of you think?'"

- "If you can tell another member is ready and willing to share, you can invite her to jump in: 'Alex, I can see you are ready to jump in. What do you think?'"

It's important to invite everyone into the conversation, O'Dell believes, because "there can't be discussion when only one person is contributing. While some people are eager to share their thoughts and opinions, others like time to process and prepare what they want to say. Tapping into everyone's natural tendency to want to be accepted leads to the most interesting discussion."

If you or others in your group are uncomfortable trying to redirect the conversation away from someone who's talking too much, you might not say anything to the perpetrator. Yet if everyone sits quietly while one or two people talk nonstop, the group's long-term best interest is not served. In most cases, using O'Dell's recommended techniques will ease the discussion away from a conversation hog and direct it back to everyone else. However, if you have a serial offender in your club, she may be more likely to change her ways if someone she feels close to in the group pulls her aside for a private conversation about her habits.

WHEN YOU'RE NOT THE ONE IN CHARGE

IT'S LIKELY THAT you'll participate in more conversations than you moderate in your mother-daughter book club. What can you do, when the tables are turned, to ensure that you can contribute to the conversation?

- Remember what it's like to be in the leader's shoes. Don't interrupt or try to lead the conversation yourself.
- Listen attentively. Really pay attention to what others in your group have to say, and look for opportunities to contribute.

- Answer questions briefly but thoughtfully. Let others in the group know why you think a character could have been more developed, or what you found appealing about the magic in a fantasy book.

- Ask questions, too. If you would like someone to clarify a point or explain in more detail, ask her to tell you more.

- Illustrate your points with short examples from personal experience. It's often easier for people to understand your ideas if you give them a point of reference.

- Keep your remarks related to the topic. Don't go off on a tangent about an experience you had in the grocery store last weekend unless it relates directly to the story you've read.

- Sit back, relax, and have fun. Soon enough it will be your job to lead the discussion again. Until then, enjoy yourself, and you'll help to create a pleasant experience for everyone in your group.

Discussion Questions That Will Work for Most Books

Here's a list of general discussion questions that will help you out if you don't have time to search for reading guides or if you can't find one relevant to your book selection.

- What did you enjoy about this book?

- What have you read that is similar?

- What do you think the author was trying to accomplish with this novel?

- Who was your favorite character? What did you appreciate about her?

- What does the main character believe in? What is she willing to fight for?

- At the end of the book, do you feel hope for the characters?

- What would you do if you were in the main character's position?

- What are the most important relationships in the book?

- What makes a minor character memorable?

- Describe one of your favorite scenes.

- Are any of the events in the book relevant to your own life?

- Was the story credible? Were the characters credible?

- Did you find any flaws in the book?

▶

▶

- What do you think will be your lasting impression of the book? Do you think you'll still remember it a year from now, or will it leave only a vague impression in your mind?

- Was the time period important to the story?

- Did you feel the author provided enough background so you could understand the historical setting?

- What else struck you as good or bad about the book?

- Were you glad you read this book?

- Would you recommend it to a friend?

- Did this book make you want to read more work by this author?

Questions for the person who chose the book:

- What made you want to read it?

- What made you suggest it to the group for discussion?

- Did it live up to your expectations? Why or why not?

- Are you sorry/glad that you suggested it to the group?

10
SHOULD YOU PICK A THEME?

> " I think that reading the same book as my daughter opens up an interesting dialogue between us. It is a great opportunity to use the experience as a teaching tool, as well as the chance to get to know my 'tween' as her peers know her. "
>
> —Melissa Halloran
> "BOOK CHICKS" MOTHER-DAUGHTER BOOK CLUB,
> ST. PETERS, MISSOURI

WHAT IS A THEME?

WHEN ALL THE books you choose to read in your mother-daughter book club have a certain connection to each other, you are reading according to a theme. A theme can create a specific focus in your group, and you can change it anytime you want. You can choose a different theme for each year that you meet, or you can pick a theme only once, then decide on a different way to select your books.

WHY CHOOSE A THEME?

DEBORAH ALVAREZ, AN elementary school librarian in Beaverton, Oregon, says she likes to choose themes for her reading groups because it "keeps rich discussion going, and it provides an opportunity to reach back and discuss previous books the students have read." What are other advantages to having a theme for your reading? A theme can:

- Help you go more in-depth into one topic
- Show you many different sides to one issue
- Teach you something about your own ethnic or cultural history
- Help you learn more about a specific author
- Let you investigate award-winning books

Of course, a theme also limits your book choices, and it may be more difficult to find enough titles for your group to read over the course of a year or more. A knowledgeable youth librarian or children's manager in a bookstore may be able to help you find age level–appropriate titles.

POSSIBLE THEMES TO CONSIDER

ALMOST ANY AREA of interest that you can think of can be considered for a book club theme. Here are a few examples you may want to think about:

The Immigrant Experience

America the melting pot has seen waves of immigrants arrive on different shores and from different countries over the years. Books that look at the experience through the eyes of new arrivals can build a picture of their lives in this country. Here are a few titles to start with:

- *Walk Across the Sea,* by Susan Fletcher: Set in the late 1880s, when Chinese immigrants were expelled from Crescent City, California.

- *Kira-Kira,* by Cynthia Kadohata: A Japanese American family moves to Georgia in the 1950s.

- *Brooklyn Doesn't Rhyme,* by Joan Blos: An eleven-year-old girl tells stories of her Polish/Jewish immigrant family in New York City during the early 1900s.

- *Esperanza Rising,* by Pam Muñoz Ryan: Thirteen-year-old Esperanza moves from Mexico to California and goes to work in the agricultural industry during the Depression.

- *Lily's Crossing,* by Patricia Reilly Giff: A young girl whose father is fighting in World War II befriends a boy who has fled Hungary.

Ethnic or Race Studies and World Cultures

If you belong to a specific race or ethnic group, you may want to focus on books about the experiences of others in your group. Or you may want to mix books from different groups so you can get an idea of many different cultures, including your own. Titles to consider include:

- *Roll of Thunder, Hear My Cry,* by Mildred Taylor: A story about the hard life of an African American family of sharecroppers.

- *Letters from Rifka,* by Karen Hesse: Modeled on the story of the author's great-aunt, who traveled from a Jewish community in the Ukraine to Ellis Island.

- *Homeless Bird,* by Gloria Whelan: A thirteen-year-old girl in India is wedded to a sickly boy so that his family can get her dowry and make a pilgrimage to healing waters where he can bathe. After her husband's family abandons her when he dies, she has to learn to make her own way in life.

- *Sold,* by Patricia McCormick: A thirteen-year-old Nepalese girl believes she is going to the city to work and earn money for her poor family, but instead is sold into slavery.

- *Bat 6,* by Virginia Euwer Wolff: This story looks at racism against Japanese Americans after World War II through the eyes of girls on a baseball team.

Award Winners

Many organizations bestow yearly awards upon children's-book authors; these books, as well as published lists of previous winners' work, can provide you with many good ideas for book club selections. Here are some of the better-known awards:

- Newbery: Each year, the American Library Association gives this award to the most distinguished American children's book published the previous year.

- Young Reader's Choice Award: Established in 1940 by Seattle bookseller Harry Hartman, this award is now administered by the Pacific Northwest Library Association. Students in fourth through twelfth grades who live in the Pacific Northwest vote for their favorites. Winners are announced in mid-April each year.

- The Scott O'Dell Award for Historical Fiction: Created by the author Scott O'Dell in 1982 to encourage other writers to focus on historical fiction.

Family

When Alvarez chose family for her theme one year, she says she enjoyed talking about how the books connected and how they differed. Her selections included:

- *The Penderwicks: A Summer Tale of Four Sisters, Two Rabbits, and a Very Interesting Boy,* by Jeanne Birdsall: As the title suggests, this books is about siblings and friendships.

- *Because of Winn-Dixie,* by Kate DiCamillo: A mutt dog helps a ten-year-old girl learn how to make friends, talk with her preacher dad, and come to terms with the fact that her mother abandoned her.

- *Ida B . . . and Her Plans to Maximize Fun, Avoid Disaster, and (Possibly) Save the World,* by Katherine Hannigan: A home-schooled only child must attend public school when her mother gets cancer.

Historical Time Periods

You may want to find out what the girls will be studying in history at school and look for historical fiction that can help bring that part of the past to life. Check with a school librarian to find great fiction from a multitude of times past. Here's a list of titles from different time periods and parts of the world to get you started:

- *Caddie Woodlawn,* by Carol Ryrie Brink: Pioneer life in Wisconsin during the mid-1800s is revealed through the eyes of Caddie, a tomboy who is modeled after the author's grandmother.

- *Catherine Called Birdy,* by Karen Cushman: We see medieval life in thirteenth-century England through the eyes of the fourteen-year-old heroine, the daughter of a minor nobleman.

- *Samurai Shortstop,* by Alan Gratz: This story takes place in Japan in the late 1800s at a time when ancient traditions were being replaced by modern ones.

- *The Kite Rider,* by Geraldine McCaughrean: A twelve-year-old boy in China protects his widowed mother and works in a circus en route to the court of the Mongol Kublai Khan during the late 1200s.

- *I Am the Mummy Heb-Nefert,* by Eva Bunting: This book explores the ancient world of Egypt as it tells the story of the pharaoh's brother's wife.

One Specific Author

You might consider choosing books by one author who has written several books in the same genre. Here are a few authors to consider, along with the titles of some of their books:

- Richard Peck has written many books about small-town American life in the late 1800s and early 1900s. They are smart and funny and attractive to readers of all ages. His titles include *A Long Way from Chicago, A Year Down Yonder, Fair Weather,* and *The Teacher's Funeral.*

- Sharon Creech writes coming-of-age stories that will resonate with young girls through early adolescence and their moms, including *Bloomability, Chasing Redbird, Granny Torrelli Makes Soup,* and *Walk Two Moons.*

- Roald Dahl created fantastical situations for children who were being taken advantage of, and he made them the stars of their own lives. Some of his most-loved titles include *Charlie and the Chocolate Factory, Matilda, James and the Giant Peach,* and *The BFG.*

- Shannon Hale has mastered the art of giving us insight into classic fairy tales by retelling them from the heroine's point of view. In *The Goose Girl, Rapunzel's Revenge, The Book of a Thousand Days,* and *Princess Academy,* the girls rescue themselves.

- Roland Smith places many of his characters in exotic places, like Burma, Kenya, and Nepal, as they encounter interesting challenges, such as escaping from kidnappers by riding on elephants, exploring caves, and climbing mountains. His books include *Elephant Run, Thunder Cave, Peak,* and *Zach's Lie.*

Nonfiction

When you want to explore a topic like careers for women or challenges that teen girls deal with, such as body-image issues, you can look for collections that talk about real people facing these same struggles. Try some of these titles:

- *Firestarters: 100 Job Profiles To Inspire Young Women,* by Kelly Beatty and Dale Salvaggio Bradshaw: This guide to career exploration profiles one hundred women and their careers, including details of what they do at work, what they did to prepare for their jobs, and what they like and dislike about them.

- *Red: The Next Generation of American Writers—Teenage Girls—on What Fires Up Their Lives Today,* by Amy Goldwasser: Teenage girls talk with honest voices about issues facing them in their everyday lives.

- *If I'd Known Then: Women in Their 20s and 30s Write Letters to Their Younger Selves,* by Ellyn Spragins: It's easy to think that confident, successful women have always felt this way, yet these stories share the insecurities and doubts the writers felt as girls. Young readers see many of the same issues they may deal with in their lives, and may see possibilities for a different future.

- *Body Drama: Real Girls, Real Bodies, Real Issues, Real Answers,* by Nancy Amanda Redd: Images of the "perfect" female body bombard us every day and give us little information about what real bodies look like, feel like, or smell like. This book of photographs and information was written by a Miss America swimsuit competition winner to help girls find and appreciate their own beauty.

Memoirs

Some of my favorite selections in my book clubs over the years have been memoirs and diaries. When you read about someone's life as he or she tells the story, you not only get an understanding of the person, but may also get a perspective of the times the author lived in. Roald Dahl's *Boy* is a good example of an impactful memoir; it has been on the reading list for both of my mother-daughter book clubs, and we have read it several times as a family as well. It's laugh-out-loud hilarious in places, but it also shows the reader a glimpse inside several British boarding schools for boys in the 1920s and '30s. You also learn about common medical practices and automobiles of the day. Other good titles in this theme include:

- *Red Scarf Girl,* by Ji-Li Jiang: A story about growing up during China's Cultural Revolution.

- *Zlata's Diary: A Child's Life in Wartime Sarajevo,* by Zlata Filipovic: See the war in Sarajevo through the eyes of an eleven-year-old girl.

- *Anne Frank: The Diary of a Young Girl:* This must-read historical diary chronicles Anne's experience hiding from the Nazis with her family in Amsterdam.

- *The Freedom Writers Diary: How a Teacher and 150 Teens Used Writing To Change Themselves and The World Around Them,* by Erin Gruwell: Modern teens from a disadvantaged high school in Los Angeles talk about the challenges they face daily.

- *West with the Night,* by Beryl Markham: From her childhood in Africa to her days as a bush pilot for elephant hunters to her first-ever female solo flight, from Europe to North America, Markham captivates readers with stories of her adventurous life.

Good Books for Boys, Too!

If you also have a son, you may want to suggest books for him to read, even if he's not in a book club of his own. The following is a list compiled from librarian recommendations, including those of Chris Houchens, who leads a father-son group at the Charleston Carnegie Public Library, in Charleston, Illinois.

AGES SEVEN AND EIGHT

- *The Adventures of Sir Lancelot the Great,* by Gerald Morris
- *Alvin Ho: Allergic to Girls, School, and Other Scary Things,* by Lenore Look
- *Attaboy Sam,* by Lois Lowry
- *The End of the Beginning,* by Avi
- *The Field Guide,* by Holly Black
- *James and the Giant Peach,* by Roald Dahl
- *The Real Thief,* by William Steig
- *Stink: The Incredible Shrinking Kid,* by Megan McDonald
- *Stone Fox,* by John Reynolds Gardiner
- *Stuart Little,* by E. B. White

AGES NINE AND TEN

- *A Long Way from Chicago,* by Richard Peck
- *Artemis Fowl,* by Eoin Colfer
- *Bud, Not Buddy,* by Christopher Paul Curtis

▶

- *Frindle* and *Room One: A Mystery or Two,* by Andrew Clements

- *The Homework Machine,* by Dan Gutman

- *Lawn Boy,* by Gary Paulsen

- *Maniac Magee,* by Jerry Spinelli

- *My Side of the Mountain,* by Jean Craighead George

- *The Mysterious Benedict Society,* by Trenton Lee Stewart

- *The Phantom Tollbooth,* by Norman Juster

- *Poppy,* by Avi

- *Shiloh,* by Phyllis Reynolds Naylor

- *Shredderman: Secret Identity,* by Wendelin Van Draanen

- *Sideways Stories from Wayside School,* by Louis Sachar

- *The Whipping Boy,* by Sid Fleischman

AGES ELEVEN TO THIRTEEN

- *Al Capone Does My Shirts,* by Gennifer Choldenko

- *Among the Hidden,* by Margaret Peterson Haddix

- *The City of Ember,* by Jeanne DuPrau

- *Crash,* by Jerry Spinelli

- *Diary of a Wimpy Kid,* by Jeff Kinney

- *The Giver,* by Lois Lowry

- *Harris and Me* and *Hatchet,* by Gary Paulsen
- *Holes,* by Louis Sachar
- *Hoot,* by Carl Hiaasen
- *The Lightning Thief,* by Rick Riordan
- *The London Eye Mystery,* by Siobhan Dowd
- *Shakespeare Bats Cleanup,* by Ron Koertge
- *Silverwing,* by Kenneth Oppel
- *Skeleton Man,* by Joseph Bruchac
- *Wednesday Wars,* by Gary Schmidt

AGES FOURTEEN AND UP

- *Acceleration,* by Graham McNamee
- *The Bourne Identity, The Bourne Supremacy,* and *The Bourne Ultimatum,* by Robert Ludlum
- *Dracula,* by Bram Stoker
- *Fat Kid Rules the World,* by K. L. Going
- *Fighting Ruben Wolfe,* by Markus Zusak
- *Frankenstein,* by Mary Shelley
- *The Hunger Games,* by Suzanne Collins
- *Monster,* by Walter Dean Myers
- *Neverwhere, Good Omens,* and *American Gods,* by Neil Gaiman
- *The Road of the Dead,* by Kevin Brooks

▶

- *Reservation Blues,* by Sherman Alexie

- *The Shining,* by Stephen King

- *Timeline,* by Michael Crichton

- *Twisted,* by Laurie Halse Anderson

- *Whale Talk,* by Chris Crutcher

If boys are not very interested in reading, Houchens says he recommends books that might pique their interest, such as those by Mike Lupica, which focus on sports, or *Star Wars: The Thrawn Trilogy,* by Timothy Zahn, for older boys. He also suggests graphic novels. "Frank Miller's *Sin City* and *300* are popular choices," says Houchens. "Many classic novels and stories have been and are being transformed into graphic novels, like Brian Jacques' *Redwall*. Art Spiegelman's *Maus* would be an example of a graphic novel that challenges the reader by putting historical events into new perspectives."

Part 2

TURNING THE PAGE: KEEPING YOUR CLUB THRIVING

11
TAKE A FIELD TRIP

" I am so fortunate that my daughter and I belong to a mother-daughter book club. Not only do I get to read (and sometimes reread) terrific books, but I also enjoy hearing what she and her friends think about the stories and the characters. I feel like I am getting to know my daughter better through our book club discussions, and I think it is definitely bringing us closer. Participating in a mother-daughter book club is also a wonderful way for us to share our love of reading! "

—Julie Peterson

MECHANICSBURG, PENNSYLVANIA

OUT OF THE ROUTINE AND INTO THE FIELD

WHETHER YOU'RE LONG past college or merely long past second grade, field trips probably hold a special place in your heart. Field trips in school can spark the imagination, encourage further learning on a topic, and energize a group. On top of that, they can be just plain fun. I still remember my grade-school field trip to the Louisiana plantation home where John James Audubon created many of his famous bird paintings, and the trip I took in high school to the French Quarter in New Orleans. Both fostered a lifelong love of the places I visited, and inspired me to keep learning more.

Taking field trips with your mother-daughter book club will let you reap all the same benefits that school field trips offer. Plus, you may also find new insights into the books you read and forge closer ties with others in your group. You needn't schedule a field trip for every book you read; too much of any format can be tiring after it becomes routine. What you're looking for instead are a few well-timed outings or other activities each year to keep interest high and reading fun. You could plan outings any time of the year, but holidays or other time off from school seems to especially lend itself to nontraditional gatherings.

BUT I DON'T HAVE TIME TO PLAN A FIELD TRIP

FIELD TRIPS DON'T necessarily require a lot of planning, but getting the timing right may require advance thought on your part. For example, the girls in Mindy's book club heard about the movie adaptation of *The Sisterhood of the Traveling Pants* when they saw a preview of upcoming films.

"The girls *loved* the book," says Mindy, "and they couldn't wait to see the movie when it came out. They particularly liked the idea that girls could strengthen their relationship with each other through a common piece of clothing. So they purchased a skirt that they passed around, similar to the way the characters in the book passed around a pair of jeans."

WHAT QUALIFIES AS A FIELD TRIP?

ALMOST ANYTHING THAT takes you out of your normal routine and helps you gain a new perspective on what you've read can be considered a field trip. If you look for opportunities to extend the learning and the bonding, you'll start to see them crop up everywhere. Here are a few ideas to get the ball rolling for you:

- See a new-release film version of a book you read—search for previews to find out when a title will start playing.

- Visit a restaurant—many ethnic restaurants feature waiters in traditional clothing, photos of the homeland on the wall, and ethnic music, as well as food that gives you a taste of what's on the menu for characters in a book.

- Attend a stage production—children's theaters and community theaters in your area may offer adaptations of children's books each season.

- Visit a museum—scratch the surface just a bit, and who knows what you'll come up with? You'll find museums dedicated to the usual (sports, crafts, and science) and the not-so-usual (hats, advertising, vortexes). You can also watch for special traveling exhibits that showcase the work of artists from a certain country or a specific historical era.

- Go to a bookstore or library—look on the shelves for staff recommendations to add to your future reading list.

- Travel to a historical site—read a historical–fiction novel set in your area; then take a trip to a local historical society or pioneer museum to get a taste for life in the old days.

- See sites around the town—visit parks, public fountains, churches, synagogues . . . the opportunities for book tie-ins are boundless.

MIX IT UP FOR A STAY-AT-HOME TRIP

YOU DON'T EVEN have to leave your normal meeting place to take a field trip—just change your routine. When Madeleine chose to read *Millions* for our book club, our family had already seen the movie on the big screen, but it was no longer playing at theaters. So we rented a copy instead. To make it work, we needed to make a few adjustments to fit the movie into our regular book club schedule.

First we moved our meeting from Thursday night after school to Sunday afternoon. Then we looked for other ways to tie in a group activity. That was easy with *Millions:* The book mentions a companion website, www.totallysaints.com. We emailed the link to everyone in our book club and asked that they check out the games and questionnaires there before we met. We made lasagna for dinner, because it matched a special dinner described in the book, and we served sticky toffee pudding, an English dessert we thought everyone would like. By the time we all settled down in our family room to watch the movie, we were relaxed and ready for an evening's entertainment.

As the movie ended, many of the moms (including me!) wiped away a few tears and said we thought the ending was bittersweet. In contrast, the girls simply thought it was sweet. We discussed differences between the book and the movie, and why we thought Frank Cottrell Boyce—who wrote the book and the screenplay—changed the things he did. It all inspired a serious conversation about human values, lightened up with an entertaining series of activities.

SO MANY MOVIES, SO LITTLE TIME

SEEING A MOVIE at home is one of the easiest ways to take a field trip. Many classic children's books have been made into movies over the years, one of the earliest being *The Wizard of Oz*, in 1939. With so many great book-movie combinations to choose from, you could easily pick one or two a year and never run out of options for as long as your group is together. Here are a few suggestions by age group to get you started:

Early Readers

- *Because of Winn-Dixie,* by Kate DiCamillo
- *Charlie and the Chocolate Factory, James and the Giant Peach,* and *Matilda,* by Roald Dahl
- *Charlotte's Web* and *Stuart Little,* by E. B. White
- *Ella Enchanted,* by Gail Carson Levine
- *The Wizard of Oz,* by L. Frank Baum

Middle Readers

- *Cheaper by the Dozen,* by Frank Bunker Gilbreth
- *The Golden Compass,* by Phillip Pullman
- *Holes,* by Louis Sachar
- *Hoot,* by Carl Hiaasen
- *Huckleberry Finn* and *Tom Sawyer,* by Mark Twain
- *Millions,* by Frank Cottrell Boyce
- *Nancy Drew Mysteries,* by Carolyn Keene
- *Peter Pan,* by James M. Barrie
- *The Princess Diaries,* by Meg Cabot
- *The Secret Garden,* by Frances Hodgson Burnett

- *Sisterhood of the Traveling Pants,* by Ann Brashares
- *Tuck Everlasting,* by Natalie Babbitt

Advanced Readers

- *In the Time of the Butterflies,* by Julia Alvarez
- *Little Women,* by Louisa May Alcott
- *Pride and Prejudice, Sense and Sensibility,* and *Emma,* by Jane Austen
- *Speak,* by Laurie Halse Anderson
- *To Kill a Mockingbird,* by Harper Lee

MOVIES ABOUT AUTHORS

- *Becoming Jane,* about Jane Austen
- *Finding Neverland,* about J. M. Barrie
- *Miss Potter,* about Beatrix Potter

THE PLAY'S THE THING

WHEN MY OLDEST daughter, Madeleine, was in fifth grade, we read *Anne Frank: The Diary of a Young Girl.* The moms in our group knew Anne's story was a lot for ten- and eleven-year-old girls to take in, and we wanted to do something that would help them absorb what they read. So we booked tickets to a production based on the book at a local children's theater.

The play brought Anne's words on the page to life. When the curtain fell, we all wanted to talk about what we had seen and read, so we headed to a nearby restaurant for dessert and discussion. Seven years later, the girls still talk about the outing as one of their favorite things about book club.

You'll find performances of great children's books adapted for community theaters and schools throughout the United States. Here are a few titles to look for:

- *Anne Frank: The Diary of a Young Girl,* by Anne Frank
- *The Giver,* by Lois Lowry
- *The Hobbit,* by J. R. R. Tolkien
- *Peter Pan,* by James M. Barrie
- *Sideways Stories from Wayside School,* by Louis Sachar
- *The Swiss Family Robinson,* by Johann David Wyss
- *The True Confessions of Charlotte Doyle,* by Avi

Each year, Denise's club attends the Shakespeare Theatre Company's Free For All in Washington, D.C., which is near their homes. Denise's family attended the event before her book club started going. When she found out the festival had a Students for Shakespeare program, she thought it would be a hit with her group.

"I like everything about going as a group," says Denise. "The plays are amazing, the preplay discussions are fascinating, and it is a great way to introduce kids to Shakespeare. It makes the kids feel smart to know something about Shakespeare—it's another little feather in their smart, young-women caps."

Denise also likes the fact that the event is free. Her club started attending when the girls were eleven or twelve, and so far they've gone five times.

GET BUY-IN BEFORE YOU SCHEDULE

THE KEY TO planning any outside activity is to get the girls involved and make sure they'll buy into whatever you decide. Don't forget that your group is a mother-*daughter* book club. By getting girls' input in deciding where your next adventure will take you, you help to make sure they don't see the book group as an obligation their mothers are enforcing.

Go on a Scavenger Hunt In Your Hometown

When my daughter Catherine and I read *Remember Me to Harold Square* with our book club, everyone in the group was intrigued by the scavenger hunt described in the book. We talked about planning something similar for summer vacation. It sounded fun to everyone, and the moms thought it would be a good way to help keep our preteen daughters more closely connected during their time off from school.

"We were sitting around my family room in February, talking about this book and all the great things the characters discovered on their scavenger hunt, when the idea came to me," says Ellen, the mom who picked the book. "I asked the group, 'What do you think about organizing something similar for us this summer?' They all thought it was a great idea. Of course, summer was still a long way off, but this gave us something to look forward to. When we met in June, we made a list of dates each of us expected to be in town and available for outings."

▶

▶

Usually the girls and moms didn't see each other at all from June until late September, when the book club started up again after summer break. We liked the idea of a scavenger hunt because it would give us a way to stay in touch. So the moms worked to come up with the list of places and activities for the girls to explore, keeping the rules simple:

- Each girl had to do at least one activity in each of four categories (food, parks, entertainment, and museums).

- At least one other girl had to be available to do it with her.

- Moms would provide transportation, but they would try to make themselves scarce so the girls could feel a bit more independent.

At the end of the summer, if everyone had tallied up enough outings, we promised there would be a prize. In the book, the main characters get to go to England if they complete their list. We couldn't do that, but we did promise the girls a weekend on the Oregon coast.

"The scavenger hunt worked even better than we expected," says Ellen. "The girls had fun discovering things they didn't know before about places to go in our town, and they were also encouraged to try new foods. When we met again for our first book club after summer, there was a lot more immediate camaraderie between everyone than in previous years. We had such a great time when we went on our prize weekend to the beach that right away we started talking about the next time we'd do something similar."

12
CONNECT WITH AN AUTHOR

" I treasure the time our mother-daughter book club provides for my daughter and me to share the books and memories made with our group. I believe it to be one of the best parts of our relationship because it provides for communication and time spent together, two things that, I realize, as my daughter ages will become even more important. I also value the strengthening of relationships between the other mothers and daughters in the group and value the opportunity to talk about thoughts and emotions with the girls while their mothers are present. "

—Jamie Osterloh
COUNCIL BLUFFS, IOWA

THE BENEFIT TO YOU

IF YOU'RE SOMEONE who thinks that meeting an author is one of the coolest things ever, you hardly need convincing that inviting an author to interact with your group is a good thing. But apart from the coolness factor, what are some other advantages of making a personal connection with an author?

- You can ask questions from the ultimate expert about your book.

- Your daughters may learn more about becoming a writer as a career choice.

- You will liven up the normal routine of your meetings.

CONNECTING IS EASIER THAN YOU THINK

CHANCES ARE, YOUR club has never invited an author to one of your meetings, either as a personal guest or as part of a phone or email conversation. But more and more authors are making an effort to connect with their readers today, and technology is making it easier than ever to bring them together with book club members, whether they live just around the corner or in another country. With just a little effort, you could find yourself playing hostess to the writer of your next book club selection.

FINDING AUTHORS WHEREVER YOU LIVE

JUST LIKE YOU, writers live everywhere—in small towns, in big cities, in foreign countries, in the neighborhood down the street. They also may visit your town to promote the release of a new book, or when their book comes out in paperback. So how do you find out about authors who live near you?

Check Local Writing Organizations

Find out if your town has a professional writers' organization. If so, you can check its website for a list of books published by members or call the membership director and ask about children's or young-adult authors who are members. See if the membership director will pass along your contact information, and ask if the author will get in touch.

Read the Book Jacket

The first time my mother-daughter book club connected with an author, we invited Laura Whitcomb, who wrote *A Certain Slant of Light,* to one of our meetings. Karen, the mom who chose the book, was reading the book jacket when she noticed that Whitcomb lived in Portland, Oregon, where our group meets. She found Whitcomb's website and sent her an invitation to our meeting, and three weeks later, the members of our club gathered around Karen's living room to talk with the author of the book we had just read.

Check Listings for Book Signings

Peruse the newspaper. Many major metropolitan newspapers print a schedule of authors who are planning to visit your area and where they will be appearing. My local newspaper, *The Oregonian,* lists all scheduled author appearances in the "Literary Calendar" section of its Sunday edition. While reading the column one day, I noticed that Zlata Filipovic, author of *Zlata's Diary: A Child's Life in Sarajevo,* would be speaking at a local bookstore to commemorate the tenth anniversary of her diary's publication. My daughter Catherine and I had read *Zlata's Diary* in our book club, and it had had a big impact on both of us. We let everyone know Zlata would be in town, then arranged to be at her reading. We all arrived early, sat in the front row, and eagerly asked questions after the presentation. When the girls saw a now-grown-up Zlata face-to-face, her words on the page suddenly meant more. They knew she was the real person who had survived bombings and seen one of her best friends killed by snipers. No amount of studying history would have had as much impact on them. A year later, the girls were thrilled to see Zlata again when she came to Portland to promote her next book. They were even more excited that she remembered them and spoke to them from the podium.

You can also check calendar listings on bookstore websites, or find out if the information is printed regularly somewhere else.

Don't Forget Libraries

Check with your library for authors who may be visiting for special children's or teens' events. Each year our public library brings in a noted children's author and a teens' author to speak and sign books. When Madeleine's group went to hear Richard Peck, who wrote *A Long Way from Chicago* and *A Year Down Yonder,* he talked about the magic of writing first lines in a book. And he told us the first line of his yet-to-be-released title, *The Teacher's Funeral.* When the book hit store shelves, we picked it up to read and were transported back to that auditorium, hearing Peck speak the opening line himself. It was as though he were reading directly to us.

Check the Internet

Many authors maintain websites, blogs, and Facebook pages where you may find a schedule of where they'll be appearing in the next few months. They might also say they're willing to talk to you by phone during your meeting, or they may be happy to answer questions you email them in advance. Then you can read your questions and answers during your regular meeting. Also, many publishers maintain a listing of where the authors of their books will be traveling.

Look for Opportunities Everywhere

Keep your radar on. Sheila's group, in Bellevue, Washington, was able to host author Kirby Larson in Sheila's home. Larson's book, *Hattie Big Sky,* was a good choice for Sheila's club of ten- and eleven-year-olds to read, and Sheila knew the author's daughter, who worked with Sheila's husband. So she sent Larson an email asking her to join them for a book club meeting. Her group was thrilled when it all came together. "The moms were all giddy-excited about this," says Sheila. "It was a great opportunity to pick an author's brain and find out why she wrote certain things into the book."

Sheila also says her group asked Larson questions about the writing process, and that the girls were especially fascinated by how stories are written. While her club hasn't hosted another author since then, it may be just a matter of time. "Every time I pick up a new book from a local author, I think about whether it would be a good book club choice; it's opened up that idea to me," Sheila says.

SCHEDULING AN AUTHOR TO ATTEND YOUR MEETING ELECTRONICALLY

DON'T BE DISCOURAGED if you don't find a local author who can meet personally with your group, or even a traveling author whose book signing you can attend. There's still the possibility that you can connect by phone or email. Look for information on writers who are willing to meet electronically, by checking authors' and publishers' websites. Best-selling authors, as well as newcomers, may be willing to connect with groups electronically in one of two ways:

- By answering a list of questions emailed in advance.
- By talking to the group in person over a speakerphone.

When you send a list of questions by email before your meeting, you allow the author to fit your group into her schedule more easily. She can compose answers to send your group whether she's at home or traveling. But you may miss the feel of a personal connection you get when you actually hear her voice over the phone line. A phone connection will give you more of a personal feel for the author, but you may have trouble communicating as a group on a speakerphone.

AUTHORS LIKE CONNECTING, TOO

As I MENTIONED before, authors today are frequently looking to make a connection with their readers, so they may appreciate getting invitations from groups. Author Heather Vogel Frederick, who often visits with mother-daughter book clubs, says, "Talking with one's audience offers a unique opportunity to enrich and extend the conversation that every book begins between author and reader. I genuinely enjoy spending time with the 'tween' age group I write for. I love their enthusiasm and delight and honesty and curiosity. I love answering their questions and offering encouragement and advice."

You can't find out if an author will connect with your group if you don't get in touch. Here's a partial list of children's and teens' authors who say they're willing for mother-daughter book clubs to call or email them, or possibly to attend meetings when they are nearby:

AUTHOR: Elise Broach
BOOKS: *Masterpiece* and *Shakespeare's Secret*
CONNECT BY: email or in person preferred; phone possible
WEBSITE: www.elisebroach.com
CONTACT INFO: hidinghoover@optonline.net

AUTHOR: Kim Culbertson
BOOK: *Songs for a Teenage Nomad*
CONNECT BY: email, phone, or in person
WEBSITE: www.kimculbertson.com
CONTACT INFO: contactkim@kimculbertson.com

AUTHOR: Katie Davis
BOOK: *The Curse of Addy McMahon*
CONNECT BY: email, in person, phone, or video chat
WEBSITE: www.katiedavis.com
CONTACT INFO: katiedavis@katiedavis.com

AUTHOR: Susan Fletcher
BOOKS: *Shadow Spinner* and *Alphabet of Dreams*
CONNECT BY: email or phone
WEBSITE: www.susanfletcher.com
CONTACT INFO: susanfletcher@centurytel.net

AUTHOR: Heather Vogel Frederick
BOOKS: *The Mother-Daughter Book Club* series, *The Voyage of Patience Goodspeed,* and *Spy Mice* series
CONNECT BY: email, in person, or phone
WEBSITE: www.heathervogelfrederick.com
CONTACT INFO: contact through website

AUTHOR: Christina Hamlett
BOOKS: *Movie Girl, Awesome Plays for Teens & Tweens*
CONNECT BY: email
WEBSITE: www.authorhamlett.com
CONTACT INFO: contact through website

AUTHOR: Ellen Klages
BOOKS: *The Green Glass Sea* and *White Sands, Red Menace*
CONNECT BY: email
WEBSITE: www.ellenklages.com
CONTACT INFO: ellen@ellenklages.com

AUTHOR: Kirby Larson
BOOK: *Hattie Big Sky*
CONNECT BY: email or phone
WEBSITE: www.kirbylarson.com
CONTACT INFO: kirby@kirbylarson.com

AUTHOR: Ingrid Law
BOOK: *Savvy*
CONNECT BY: email or phone
WEBSITE: www.ingridlaw.com
CONTACT INFO: ingrid@ingridlaw.com

AUTHOR: Kristin O'Donnell Tubb
BOOK: *Autumn Winifred Oliver Does Things Different*
CONNECT BY: email, in person, or phone
WEBSITE: www.kristintubb.com
CONTACT INFO: ktubb@comcast.net

AUTHOR: Mary E. Pearson
BOOKS: *The Adoration of Jenna Fox* and *A Room on Lorelei Street*
CONNECT BY: email or in person
WEBSITE: www.marypearson.com
CONTACT INFO: mary@marypearson.com

AUTHOR: Renée Rosen
BOOK: *Every Crooked Pot*
CONNECT BY: in person or phone preferred; email possible
WEBSITE: www.reneerosen.com
CONTACT INFO: everycrookedpot@gmail.com

AUTHOR: Tammar Stein
BOOKS: *Light Years* and *High Dive*
CONNECT BY: email or phone
WEBSITE: www.tammarstein.com
CONTACT INFO: tammarstein@hotmail.com

AUTHOR: Nancy Werlin
BOOKS: *Impossible, The Rules of Survival,* and *The Killer's Cousin*
CONNECT BY: email, in person, phone, or Skype
WEBSITE: www.nancywerlin.com
CONTACT INFO: nancy@nancywerlin.com

AUTHOR: Laura Whitcomb
BOOKS: *A Certain Slant of Light* and *The Fetch*
CONNECT BY: email, in person, or phone
WEBSITE: www.laurawhitcomb.com
CONTACT INFO: contact through website

Don't take it personally if an author says no to your request. So much depends on her schedule, her other obligations, differences in time zones, and other factors that have nothing to do with you and your club. Just keep trying, and resolve to find someone else who can make the connection.

The Dos and Don'ts of
Connecting with Authors

Always keep in mind that you want the author to feel comfortable when she's interacting with your group. If she is invited to attend your regular meeting in person, include her in your normal activities. Ask whether she has time for extras, like coming early for a meal or crafts and other social activities. If you are connecting by phone, make sure background noise is kept to a minimum so she can hear well, and have each person who speaks identify herself before she makes a comment or asks a question.

Here are some other pointers that will help you strike upon just the right tone to put the author at ease and plan a successful event from conception to finish.

DO:

- Respect an author's time and realize she is doing you a favor by connecting with your mother-daughter book club, when her calendar is probably littered with personal and professional commitments.

- Research her biographical information. Find out about other books she's written, where she lives, and her other interests if you can.

- Think of questions in advance. Go beyond the obvious—ask questions that show you really read her work.

- Listen to what the author has to say. You may be tempted to jump in with your own opinion, but the

▶

author is the expert. Since you invited her, show you're willing to learn from her.

- Keep time-zone considerations in mind. If she lives in Massachusetts and you live in California, don't ask if she can chat by phone when your group meets at 7:00 PM. Ask instead about convenient times for her, and then work around them as best you can.

- Ask to take a photo with her if you see her in person, either at a bookstore or at your regular meeting.

DON'T:

- Ask for free copies of an author's book to read in advance. If you'll be meeting her in person, buy a copy of her book ahead of time so she can inscribe it personally.

- Act as though you're doing the author a favor by asking her to meet with you. Even if you all bought her book and you're all adoring fans, it's not the career equivalent of her being chosen to be part of Oprah's Book Club.

- Come off as a stalker. Showing up on an author's door step to plead your case may have just the opposite effect you'd like it to. Authors expect their private lives to be respected.

- Say bad things about the writing or the book when you meet. That doesn't mean you have to pretend you liked everything about what you read. Try asking questions about the things you didn't like, so you can get a better feel for what the author was trying to say.

▶

- Forget that a writer is a professional. She likely works hard to produce and market every book she writes.

- Expect privileged treatment at an author's bookstore reading just because you're a group. Everyone at the reading is attending because they want to hear the author speak and possibly get her to sign a book.

13
BRING IN AN EXPERT

" Most children pass through the 'age of silence.' Dialogue that opens up in a mother-daughter book club is a wonderful bridge of communication over this silence. "

—Eileen Faradji
MIAMI, FLORIDA

INVITING NONAUTHOR GUESTS

AUTHORS AREN'T THE only guests you can invite to join you at a book cub gathering. You can also liven up your meetings by inviting an expert on a topic you're reading about. How does an expert differ from an author? An author can help you learn more about the book itself, and can tell you everything you'd like to know about the experience of writing it. An expert can help you learn more about the topic covered in a book, or a related topic.

EXTENDING THE EXPERIENCE

WHEN YOU THINK in terms of inviting an expert, as opposed to an author, you also extend the possibilities of people who may be qualified to talk about a specific area. In most cases, one person is the author of a book, but many, many people may be experts on what the book is about. Thinking about inviting an expert also gives you flexibility when deciding on your focus. You can look for something you'd like to know more about in a book you choose to read, or you can first pick a subject that you want to learn more about, then find a book and an expert to fit.

In Inez's book club, the moms had already talked about a topic they thought was important for their girls to know more about; then they made a connection with the book they chose to read and arranged for a visitor to join them. The subject? Manners.

"One of the moms was saying how she always sends presents to her nieces and nephews, and that she never knows if they liked what they got, because they don't write thank-you notes," says Inez. "That got us talking about how no one is teaching youngsters to say 'please' and 'thank you,' or to hold doors open for people anymore." When the group chose to read *The New York Stories of Edith Wharton*—a book about upper-class society in New York during the 1800s—the moms remembered their earlier discussion on manners.

"Another mom and I decided this would be a good chance to show the girls that it's not so hard to be polite, and that it's a show of respect for other people," Inez says. One of the moms in her group knew an older woman who had belonged to several social clubs when she lived in New York. As a guest, she provided a connection to the book's setting and to the topic of etiquette, so the moms decided to create a special event by inviting her to a meeting.

Inez says they set the stage by having everyone dress up for book club as though they were attending a tea party, a departure from their normal blue jeans, T-shirts, and tennis shoes. "We made tea and had finger sandwiches and petits fours, got scones from a local bakery, and had several kinds of tea," says Inez. "Everyone talked about the stories we liked best in the book. Then our guest had us play fun games to learn manners, such as how to set a formal table and how to introduce one another properly; she even handed out an etiquette quiz. We all learned something and had fun, too. And, of course, each of the girls sent a handwritten thank-you note to our guest afterward."

WHO IS AN EXPERT?

AN EXPERT CAN be defined as someone who has comprehensive and authoritative knowledge of or skill in a particular area. The woman who visited Inez's club qualifies as an expert because she has both knowledge of *and* skill with manners. Give it a little thought, and you will probably find that many people you know are experts on some subject. It may be your neighbor down the street or a teacher in your daughter's school or even the veterinarian where you take your pet for checkups. The trick is finding the right person to talk about the specific subject you want to cover.

MATCHING THE BOOK TO THE EXPERT

ONE WAY TO choose an expert to invite to your club meeting is to think about something you would like to know more about, then find someone who can speak on the topic. How will you find these experts? Experts are all around us, although we probably don't think of the people we know that way. To you, they may be simply a neighbor or a friend or a family member, but at work they may be practicing some area of expertise every day that ties in to what you are seeking.

A simple brainstorming exercise can help you come up with a list of specialties for everyone you know. First, find out about the expertise in your own group of moms. In my groups, moms know a lot about diet and nutrition, heart health, writing, medical research, teaching, sewing, knitting, playing mah-jongg, playing tennis, nursing, and advertising. If we all sat down to brainstorm together, we would probably discover a few more specialized areas that one of us could speak about.

From there, expand into your closest circle. Talk about what your spouses specialize in. In our case, they design software, draw political cartoons, sell medical equipment, manage teams of workers, and write advertising copy.

After that, discuss neighbors or friends who may have something to contribute. For example, in my neighborhood live a retired pilot, a man who works for the Drug Enforcement Administration, a psychiatrist, and a software engineer. Then make a list that also includes other people you may see often:

- Your daughters' teachers
- Your local librarian
- Your physicians
- A pastor at your church
- A trainer at your health club

Think about the expertise each of them brings to the table: A teacher or librarian may be able to talk about a historical era or local history; you may see an acupuncturist who can speak about Chinese medicine; your pastor can talk about biblical stories; your trainer can talk about healthy ways to make your body strong.

The bigger your club, the more opportunities you may have for finding a close connection to the expert you are seeking. Once you see how many possibilities exist, you can look for books that touch on the topic you would like to know more about. Ask any of the experts you have identified if they know of a book that deals with your topic. You can also ask for advice from librarians or bookstore personnel.

MATCHING THE EXPERT WITH A BOOK

IF YOU ALREADY have a book in mind, your task is identifying themes in the book and looking at creative ways to enhance them. The New York stories that Inez's book club read were not specifically about manners, but manners were a big part of society at the time, and they played a prominent role in the characters' actions.

What are some other book-topic pairings that may lend themselves to expert input? Here are a few; you will certainly be able to think of more.

- *Bat 6,* by Virginia Euwer Wolff: West Coast history, Japanese internment, baseball, World War II
- *Bloomability,* by Sharon Creech: travel, learning to speak Italian, attending boarding school

- *Fair Weather,* by Richard Peck: the many inventions introduced at the Chicago World's Fair in 1893
- *Framed,* by Frank Cottrell Boyce: famous works of art
- *Hoot,* by Carl Hiaasen: environmental issues
- *James and the Giant Peach,* by Roald Dahl: animation for movies
- *Julie of the Wolves,* by Jean Craighead George: learning survival skills
- *Light Years,* by Tammar Stein: required military service in Israel
- *Petey,* by Ben Michaelson: cerebral palsy, other disabilities
- *Red Scarf Girl,* by Ji-Li Jiang: China's Cultural Revolution
- *The Secret Life of Bees,* by Sue Monk Kidd: honey, cooking with honey
- *Sold,* by Patricia McCormick: global slave trade
- *Stargirl,* by Jerry Spinelli: playing the guitar
- *The Trumpet of the Swan,* by E. B. White: musical instruments, trumpeter swans
- *Walk Across the Sea,* by Susan Fletcher: early Chinese workers on the West Coast

EXPERT ETIQUETTE

IF YOU KNOW the expert you invite to your club meeting well, and you know she is happy to join your group to talk about a specific topic, you may be tempted to treat her as just another one of the gang. Resist the temptation. Her words will carry more weight in the discussion if she is treated like the expert she is. Remember, also, to follow the same list of dos and don'ts listed in the previous chapter for connecting with an author.

While some of the suggestions may seem too formal for working with someone you know, the tips are a good reminder that you are asking for a favor when you ask someone to give up a few hours of her time to spend with your group. Take a lesson from Inez's book club as well, and remember to send your expert a thank-you note from everyone in your group after your meeting.

Schedule a Poetry Meeting

If reading poetry is not the first thing you think of as a choice for your mother-daughter book club, neither should it be the last. Many excellent books make poetry fun and accessible for both children and adults. One of those is Shel Silverstein's classic *Where the Sidewalk Ends,* a book selected by Lisa's book club of seven- and eight-year-old daughters. Lisa says their poetry meeting prompted more participation from everyone than usual.

"I loved the incredible amount of laughing and giggling that came with reading the poems," says Lisa. "Each mom and daughter had tons of favorite poems and were eager to read them. We discussed the themes of the poems and talked about what we liked or didn't like about the illustrations."

Moms and girls also tried their own hand at writing poetry, working to create acrostic poems using each letter of their names as the first letter of one line. The group had so much fun at their meeting that they decided to read another of

▶

▶

Silverstein's collections to celebrate National Poetry Month, which is held every April.

Kenn Nesbitt, author of many collections of humorous children's poetry and creator of the popular children's-poetry website Poetry4Kids.com, says poetry is important for kids as well as adults. "For kids who are learning to read, exposing them to poetry, especially to humorous poetry, can foster a true love of reading," Nesbitt explains. "Like reading joke and riddle books, reading humorous poetry does not require a lot of effort in order to create a positive emotional response. Reading just one or two pages can make a child smile or laugh. Poems, however, usually do a better job of improving a child's vocabulary and reading skills than riddles and jokes, because of their greater length and emphasis on word selection."

Even adults can appreciate poetry geared toward children, because it may put less pressure on them to find the deeper meaning of a poem. My family and I had an experience similar to Lisa's book club's when we focused on reading poetry for a month. We each checked out books of poetry from the library, then took turns reading our favorites over dinner every night. By mixing in a few classics from Emily Dickinson, Walt Whitman, Henry Wadsworth Longfellow, and Langston Hughes with popular children's poets of today, we got an idea of how good poetry can move us in many ways.

Here are a few ideas to help you plan a poetry meeting for your mother-daughter book club. First, choose one or more books of poetry from authors sure to appeal to children and adults. In addition to Shel Silverstein's *Where the Sidewalk Ends* and his other collections, possibilities include:

- Kenn Nesbitt: *Revenge of the Lunch Ladies, My Hippo Has the Hiccups: And Other Poems I Totally Made Up,* and several other collections of poetry

- Jack Prelutsky: *A Pizza the Size of the Sun* and *It's Raining Pigs and Noodles,* plus more titles of poetry

- Robert Louis Stevenson: *A Child's Garden of Verses*

- Emily Dickinson: *The Complete Poems of Emily Dickinson*

Second, try your hand at writing poetry. Nesbitt advises you that poetry doesn't have to be about "poetic" subjects, such as nature or love. "Write about your favorite thing, or something you dislike, or something that happens to you, or how you are feeling, or something you see around you," he says.

Styles that may work best for children include:

- Acrostic: uses the letters in a name or a word to begin each line. All words in the poem relate to the person or thing that the name or word represents.

- Haiku: three lines with five syllables on the first line, seven on the second, five on the third.

- Free-form: doesn't rhyme or have a specific syllable count, but tends to have a melodic flow.

Finish your meeting on poetry by reading some of your favorite poems aloud. This will let you get into the rhythm of poetry as your voice follows the meter, and you may even find yourselves cracking up.

14
STAGE A PLAY

" We are equal members discussing wonderful literature, and at the same time we're opening a dialogue with our daughters that will last a lifetime. **"**

—Sheila Ferry
BELLEVUE, WASHINGTON

MIX IT UP WITH LIVE THEATER

CHANCES ARE, CHOOSING a play isn't top of mind when you are searching for your next mother-daughter book club selection. Reading a play, with all its stage instructions to the actors included with the text, is a different experience from reading a novel or a work of nonfiction. Plays are less likely to describe settings in detail, and more likely to focus on what the characters say and do. Yet you may find that reading a play and staging a performance with your club are a great way to introduce your girls to theater in a nonthreatening format.

BENEFITS OF PERFORMING

IN ADDITION TO adding variety to your meetings, staging a play with your mother-daughter book club offers several potential benefits to all the members of your group, including the moms. Christina Hamlett is an award-winning author who has written more than 125 plays, several of them collected in her book *Awesome Plays for Teens & Tweens*. In her extensive work with young people on the stage, Hamlett has found that "acting improves listening, diction, and communication skills; encourages teamwork, leadership, and cooperation; and provides a comfortable, non-threatening platform for discussing age-appropriate issues that impact their lives." She also believes that the stage is a tremendous forum for building confidence and self-esteem.

Inez's mother-daughter book club members performed plays from Hamlett's book when the girls ranged in age from ten to fourteen, and she says her group definitely gained from its experience. "The girls learned how to speak up instead of mumbling lines with the scripts held up in front of their faces," says Inez. "They learned how to focus on the moment and the interactions with their fellow actors, and how to make the role they were playing their very own—for instance, by speaking with an accent or using certain mannerisms to distinguish their characters from others in the play." For the moms, Inez says the experience was memorable as well, since they could see how much fun the girls were having and the confidence they were gaining from the experience.

HOW WILL YOU KNOW IF YOUR GIRLS ARE OLD ENOUGH TO PERFORM?

WHEN SHOULD YOU consider staging a play with your mother-daughter book club? Hamlett points out that "theater is a natural segue from what imaginative children already do on their own in the back yard with friends, dolls, and stuffed animals." She believes confidence and maturity are bigger factors than chronological age is in deciding whether or not you want to schedule a play in your lineup.

Lisa Bany-Winters, author of *On Stage: Theatre Games and Activities for Kids,* says girls of all ages can perform at a mother-daughter book club meeting if you look for age-appropriate materials. "Younger girls may improvise or act out without a script some of the characters and situations in the book. Older girls can create a play based on the book, memorize their lines if desired, and put on an entire performance."

CHOOSING A PIECE TO PERFORM

KEEP IN MIND that just as you choose age-appropriate books for your girls to read, you will also want to choose an age-appropriate script for them to perform. Inez recommends that you consider vocabulary used in the play along with other criteria, because that will affect how well your girls will be able to read their lines. She also suggests having your girls read monologues. "If you're studying famous women in history, for example, you could have each girl read a monologue out loud for the group. This could be from an actual book of play monologues, or you could find an autobiography and turn one of the pages in the book into a mini-speech," says Inez.

As Bany-Winters notes, you can encourage a budding playwright in your group by asking her to write a short piece based on a book your group has read, or she can create an original work of her own. She also recommends that you look for stories with a number of interesting characters and lots of dialogue. "*Alice in Wonderland* is a good example that has lots of fun characters, each having a conversation with Alice," says Bany-Winters. She suggests you check the nonfiction section of your library to find scripts of books that have already been adapted into easy plays to perform, such as *James and the Giant Peach* and *Peter Pan*. Such classic titles also present a familiar story for your girls to act out, and it may be easier for them to play a character they already have a mental image of.

Hamlett recommends looking at one-act plays, which may have lots of roles for your budding actors but are typically shorter and easier to stage. She agrees that finding something age appropriate is important. "For lower and middle grades, this usually takes the form of popular fairy tales or familiar characters in updated settings, as in Sleeping Beauty and Rapunzel at a beauty salon," says Hamlett. "For teenage thespians, the ability to follow more complicated plots opens the door to mysteries, light romance, parodies, and 'issue' plays that celebrate history, self-esteem, and cultural diversity."

She advises you to browse through several websites where you can find both classics and newly written plays:

- New Plays (www.newplaysforchildren.com)

- Teaching Heart (www.teachingheart.net/readerstheater.htm)
- Classics On Stage! (www.classicsonstage.com)
- The Internet Theatre Bookshop (www.stageplays.com)
- Scripts for Schools (www.scriptsforschools.com)

These sites offer low-cost or free scripts, and they may also list other logistics, like the number of characters in a play, appropriate ages, and how long you can expect the performance to last. Some of the sites also offer helpful tips for staging your performance. Hamlett says any mother-daughter book club with a more serious interest in theater should also check out the magazine *Plays,* which publishes scripts each month for lower grades, upper grades, readers' theater, and adaptations of classics.

ASSIGNING ROLES

WHEN IT CAME time to assign roles for the play they'd chosen to perform, Inez's group put the names of all the characters on slips of paper, and everyone drew a name out of a hat. She says they wanted to be fair, but they also wanted to show that members could adapt to playing a role they may not have been particularly drawn to at first. "Originally we were just going to have the girls play the female roles, and the moms would play the males. But I think it's important in theater that you push the envelope a little and allow participants to experiment with their voices and emotions to convey the characters."

You can also talk in advance about what each role will involve, so that everyone understands where her character fits in. Then have each person say which role she would like to take on.

If you have more than one person speaking up for the same role, you can draw names to choose who will get the assignment.

Another possibility Bany-Winters suggested is having each person write down three parts she would like to play. "Remind the girls that a group of actors cannot perform *The Wizard of Oz* with seven Dorothys, and that all roles are important," she says. "Try to give each girl one of the three roles she requested. If you cannot, talk with them about other solutions. Perhaps roles can be double cast, with two performances, or you can use your creativity and add fun characters, such as Dorothy's little sister."

In spite of your efforts at fairness, you may not be able to totally avoid hurt feelings if a girl doesn't get the role she prefers. But she can still have fun with the experience and learn about working well in a group if she can make the best of the role she is assigned.

What happens if a girl in your group is painfully shy and doesn't want to take on any role? First, you can encourage her to choose a small role with little stage time. It will be good practice for her, and it may help her gain confidence while learning techniques that will help her when she has to make a presentation at school. If she is still set against being onstage, Hamlett recommends that you don't push her into performing or reading out loud. "Keep in mind that there are plenty of nonacting tasks that go into a performance, such as making simple costumes, designing programs, and managing a prop box," she says. Help her to see that her contributions are valuable even when she doesn't take center stage.

PREPPING YOUR STAGE

IF YOU HAVE enough room in a home where you meet, getting the stage ready may mean simply moving couches and chairs back from the main floor area of your family room. For more space to move around, you may want to check out reserving a meeting room at your local library if you don't meet there already. Hang a sheet across a doorway to designate your behind-the-stage area, where actors will wait in the wings for their entrance cues, and dim the lights if you can.

You may want to put out a few props in advance, like a chair or two, or a small table with a flower vase if it's appropriate. Otherwise, you can simply have each actor carry any props she needs as she enters and exists the stage. Simple costumes with scarves and plain fabric draped and pinned or taped together are easy to prepare. You can also draw on paper and cut it out in shapes to create a period costume that may be harder to portray with fabric. The key is to keep it simple and easy while having fun with any preparations you make.

GET SILLY WITH WARM-UP EXERCISES

SEASONED ACTORS OFTEN do warm-up exercises before they hit the stage. They know that taking your thoughts off the performance to concentrate on a mind game or a silly action will help you banish any jitters you may have. So, too, can everyone in your mother-daughter book club benefit from a few warm-up exercises, even if you are performing only in front of each other.

Over the years, both of my daughters have enjoyed taking on theater roles for school productions. Madeleine and Catherine say that theater warm-ups are often so much fun, they play them with groups of friends at parties as well as when they are prepping for the stage. Here are some of their favorites.

Tongue Twisters

These phrases will loosen up your tongue and help you practice enunciating clearly. You will probably also loosen up your funny bone as you attempt to say them over and over while speaking faster and faster.

A MINUTE OR TWO TILL TWO

What a to do to die today

At a minute or two till two

A thing distinctly hard to say

Yet harder still to do

PETER PIPER

Peter Piper picked a peck of pickled peppers

If Peter Piper picked a peck of pickled peppers

How many pickled peppers did Peter Piper pick

PERCY PIG

Percy Pig is plump and pink

I like a plump, pink pig I think

Intimidation

This game helps you learn to project your voice and become comfortable with both physical movement and emotional expression. Have everyone stand in a circle. Person one starts by shouting someone else's name (person two) and walking toward her slowly and menacingly. Her hands are clenched, and her face looks angry as she walks. Person two needs to stand her ground without flinching, and before person one arrives in front of her, she needs to shout someone else's name and start walking slowly toward her. Person one will take person two's space in the circle. Do this until everyone has had a chance to call out someone's name and practice acting out an angry emotion, as well as being calm in the face of that emotion.

Number Up

You will learn to become more in tune with the energy and personal vibes of others in your group when you play Number Up. Start by having everyone sit in a circle and close her eyes. The object is to count up from one to ten, in no specific order. The first person says one, then someone else says two, and so on. If two people speak a number at the same time, start over with one. To avoid talking at the same time, you will have to listen with your eyes closed for clues that someone is about to speak. Do you hear someone breathe in, as though she will soon say a number? Does someone else shift her body, rustling her clothes, before she speaks? This game heightens your awareness of non-visual clues that can help you anticipate action.

Bany-Winters also recommends finding more theater games and ice-breakers in her book *On Stage: Theatre Games and Activities for Kids.*

RAISE THE CURTAIN

BEFORE YOU RAISE the curtain on your performance, you will want to make sure that each member of your group has had time to get familiar with her role. Even if you keep it simple and read your lines with a script in hand, it helps if you can practice in advance so you can perfect an accent, determine your tone of voice, or think of an action that goes along with your words.

Inez says her group wanted to fit a play into its regular monthly-meeting schedule. So the members handed out scripts and assigned roles the month before they performed. This gave them plenty of time to rehearse at home. They also prepped everyone in advance by having one of the girls talk about a few basic considerations, like not standing with your back to the audience and not blocking another character while you perform.

If you feel confident and want to perform for others, you could invite dads and other siblings to be your audience. You may also want to enlist a member of your group or another family member to record your performance on video. That way, you can all watch your drama unfold as members of the audience, as well as actors in the play.

POSTSHOW

ONCE YOUR PERFORMANCE is over, schedule a "cast party" along the lines of your group's regular book discussion. This is a great time to talk about anything you learned by acting a piece instead of just reading it. Inez's group even asked each participant what she thought her character did after the story ended.

You could also keep an eye out for a community-theater production of the play you performed. You're likely to have a whole different perspective of what you watch on the stage when you've had the chance to be up there yourself.

Create a Soundtrack for Your Mother-Daughter Book Club

When you've finished performing your play, you may want to turn your attention to another activity that will keep your creative juices flowing: creating a soundtrack for each mother-daughter pair in your group, or for your group as a whole. Songs are like poetry set to music, and choosing one or more that are significant to you can open up conversations about events or emotions that are important to each of you.

In her novel, *Songs for a Teenage Nomad*, Kim Culbertson touches on the chord that music can strike in our lives. The main character, Callie, is a teenage girl who has moved around with her mom most of her life. With each move, she

▶

turns to music to help her adjust as she tries once more to fit in, and songs she chooses have some meaning to the stage she's going through at the moment. Culbertson leads workshops in which she helps participants choose songs to create a soundtrack of their lives, then journal about them. Here are her suggestions for how you can create your own soundtrack and song journal:

- Select ten songs that have significance to both moms and daughters in some way. You can each choose ten different songs to create your individual soundtrack, or you can choose ten songs to represent your group. At the beginning of your soundtrack, include a list of the songs (as well as the name of the artist or band) that you selected.

- For each song, write a passage describing what it means to you, focusing on a scene/memory in your life that this song brings to mind. Focus on using specific detail and sensory description to *show* the memory, rather than just telling the story behind it. These entries could take the form of journal posts or poems, or could simply describe the memory as a narrative. Be creative in how you present them to each other.

- At the end of the soundtrack, include album notes that explain why you chose the songs you did for your relationship overall, and what you feel they say about you or your group.

- Design a creative CD cover for your soundtrack.

▶

If you own the music you've chosen and have access to a computer, you can complete your soundtrack by burning your songs to a CD. If you don't own the music already, you can often purchase single songs inexpensively from any of several online sources, including iTunes, Napster, and Mp3.com. Some things to consider before you begin:

- Do you want to stick to one genre, like classical, pop, rock, country, or rap, or are you just as happy to create an eclectic mix?

- Would you like the soundtrack to say something about you as a group, or as a mother and daughter? This will help you decide whether each mother-daughter pair will create its own soundtrack or if you will create one as a club.

As your girls grow, the songs that have special meaning to you and to them will likely change. To capture these changes, you can repeat this activity every few years as your girls move from elementary school to middle school to high school. When they graduate, they will have a time capsule of songs that meant a lot to them and other members of your group over the years.

15
VOLUNTEER TOGETHER

" Moms and daughters often see themselves only through the lens of that important and often tricky relationship. Being in a mother-daughter book club is great because it is an opportunity for moms and daughters to see one another as the complex people they really are, but in the most casual environment for honest communication. In talking about things we read, we talk about our hopes and fears, our passions, and what makes each of us unique. It is wonderful to know those things about people we love so much. (And the books and the snacks are pretty great, too!) "

—Denise Neary
ROCKVILLE, MARYLAND

DECIDING TO VOLUNTEER TOGETHER

UNLIKE YOUTH GROUPS such as Girl Scouts and Camp Fire, which encourage all members to embark on service projects, a mother-daughter book club has no built-in concept that will automatically make you think of volunteering as a group. You or someone else will bring up the idea because you believe the benefits are worth the time you spend.

Maybe you have volunteered for a cause yourself, or maybe you have heard of others' experiences and want to bring something similar to your group. Maybe your daughter is required to spend a certain number of hours volunteering to earn credit for a class at school. Whatever your motivation, volunteering is a commitment you make to each other, as well as to the cause you choose to serve.

BENEFITS TO YOU AND TO YOUR COMMUNITY

WHEN YOU VOLUNTEER with your daughter, you do more than contribute to a worthy cause. Heather Jack, founder of the Volunteer Family, which keeps a database that connects volunteers with projects in forty states, has volunteered extensively since she was young. Jack strongly believes that we give our children a gift when we seek out opportunities to give back to our communities. "It teaches kids self-esteem, they learn new skills, and they are able to appreciate people from different backgrounds and beliefs," she explains. "Families are able to spend quality time together, and if it's in a group situation, they are able to spend time with other people important to them as well."

CHOOSING YOUR CAUSE

SO MANY WORTHY organizations and opportunities exist, your biggest challenge after deciding to take on a volunteer project may be choosing where you want to commit your time. To start narrowing down your options, talk to the moms and daughters in your group, and take an informal survey of their interests. What issues are they passionate about? Where would they be most happy helping out? Think in broad terms at first, instead of trying to identify a specific agency. While you are certain to find service groups dedicated to many different causes, most break down into one of three umbrella categories:

- Human welfare
- Environmental welfare
- Animal welfare

Then take a look at special talents in your group. Is someone particularly good at creating art? Do several of you like to sew or knit? Would you like to cook something to advance a cause? You may discover that you all like to work outdoors, or that you want to share your passion for reading.

Your list can also include anything you would like to learn. Do you want to know more about where the water that goes down your sewer ends up, and how it contributes to an ecosystem? Do you want to learn more about how people in other countries live? Again, continue to keep your conversation broad for now.

Next, combine your interests with the type of agency you would like to help, so you can narrow down your choices a bit. Would you like to knit baby blankets for an agency serving the poor or victims of domestic abuse? Are you interested in collecting food for the hungry? Do you want to help the environment by working to clear invasive species off trails in a local park? Would you like to bake treats for an animal shelter?

Once you answer these questions and have a good idea of the type of project you can all support enthusiastically, choosing an actual agency to approach about volunteering will be much easier.

FINDING THE RIGHT PROJECT FOR YOUR GROUP

AS A LONGTIME Girl Scout leader, I've worked alongside girls as young as ten and as old as seventeen as they pulled invasive weeds on protected land for the Nature Conservancy, collected canned goods for the Oregon Food Bank, delivered meals to seniors as part of our city's Meals on Wheels program, and pounded nails to help build a home through Habitat for Humanity. As the girls grew, their interests and their abilities grew with them.

Heather Jack agrees that opportunities with service agencies will change as your girls grow older, but don't be discouraged if the agency you choose requires that your girls be older than they are to fill official volunteer positions. "If you're talking about a food pantry," says Jack, "there are usually age requirements for serving food and working in the kitchen. But younger girls can do things like assemble bag lunches and bring them into the dining room. You can even come up with a new idea for the agency. You can say something like, 'Do you mind if we try . . . ?' Be creative to work around their standard parameters for volunteering."

THREE DIFFERENT CLUBS, THREE DIFFERENT WAYS TO SERVE

MOTHER-DAUGHTER BOOK clubs around the country have found ways to successfully give time or money to causes that are important to them. Here are three stories from groups with girls ages seven to thirteen.

Addressing Literacy and Hunger at the Same Time

Sheila's book club, composed of twelve- and thirteen-year-old girls and their moms, was considering doing something together as a group, but they didn't know what they would do or when they would do it. They debated going away for a weekend or volunteering together; Sheila's "aha" moment came as she was talking to another mom at her daughter's school bus stop. What she discovered was a program that collected books to give to underprivileged children during the summer months, when they are not in school.

"Anybody who likes to read knows there's something very powerful about reading," said Sheila. "I thought it would be great if we could incorporate our love of books into our service work." The program Sheila's book club volunteered for was called Peanut Butter, Jelly, and Books, and it employed a two-pronged approach: Girls and moms would collect books to donate, then go to the community center where the summer program takes place to interact with the kids receiving the books.

"I think it's an even better connection to the service work when you actually get to meet the people you're helping," says Sheila. "The personal aspect of it is what makes an impact."

To start their project, moms and daughters collected books from family members and friends during the month of November, then brought them to Sheila's house when they met for book club. Sheila delivered them to the community center. During summer, they planned to have lunch twice with kids who were part of the program.

Sheila thinks the girls learned a lot when they saw that books aren't as accessible to most children as they are to them.

"We found out that a lot of kids who come in for the program have never been to a public library. We talked about how we all have lots of books, and we have access to lots of books, but that's not the case for everybody," she says.

Tying Service Projects in with Ideas from Books You Read

The girls in Tamie's group attend a school that advocated a new service mentality, asking each student to consider participating in projects to aid the community. The girls were in second grade when their book club decided to volunteer together the first time, and they looked for ways to tie a project in with a book they read. When they chose to read *The Hundred Dresses,* by Eleanor Estes, an opportunity presented itself. "All the girls brought one of their fanciest dresses (many brought more than one) to be donated to the shelter for domestic violence here in town," says Tamie. The daughters really enjoyed the project, so when they read *The Family Under the Bridge,* by Natalie Savage Carlson, they decided to embark on another project by making fleece blankets for local homeless shelters.

"The impact was amazing," says Tamie. "We, as a group, felt really fortunate to be able to do something that would help others. The girls, after reading *The Family Under the Bridge,* started to discuss the idea of not having a home. However, not until we started making the blankets, and really thinking and talking about all of the implications of not having a house, did it really start to soak into the girls' hearts that they should be thankful for their environment. More importantly, they learned to be more empathetic for those who are not as fortunate."

Tamie believes their projects have brought members of the group closer, and have strengthened mother-daughter bonds as well. "I think by doing the service projects, you present the opportunity to have an honest discussion about feelings, and with that you enable the group to open up their minds and hearts for what I call 'real' discussion. Based on our prior experiences, I know without a doubt we will continue to put an emphasis on giving back and assisting those in need," she says.

Turning Your Talents and Interests into a Fundraiser

When Marci's group read *Rent a Third Grader*, by B. B. Hiller, the girls were in fourth and fifth grade and the club was just starting out. The book is about a group of students who raise money to help an old police horse remain part of the community, and it inspired the girls to help their local animal shelter by organizing a bake sale.

Marci says the girls baked everything on their own: trays and trays of cookies, brownies, cupcakes, and muffins. "We advertised in the local newspaper about our bake sale, saying that all proceeds would be donated to the local animal shelter," she says. "We held it in a gym that houses all the local basketball games, and it ran from 8:30 AM to 5:00 PM. We raised about $300, and the girls presented the animal shelter with the money to help them care for stray animals."

Marci believes the project helped the group in many ways. "The girls learned how to put into action the good feelings they had from the book," she says. "They also had an opportunity to learn about each other in a different environment and see each other out in the world. Since the bake sale was local, the girls learned they had many of the same friends in common, and they established more connections amongst themselves."

Marci believes the moms took away something from the project, too. "They got to spend time with the girls and see their individual personalities and passions come out, and they were able to observe their own daughters interacting with new people," she says.

PLAN TO SUCCEED

WHILE NOT ALL of these projects were simple, they all had one thing in common: They had buy-in from members of the group. If you are really excited about a project that is important to you, it may be easy to overlook polite and subtle hints from others that they are not totally onboard. Moms and girls alike can be swept away by enthusiasm from someone in the group without being sure they really want to participate in the project: They may agree with the project but find that the timing isn't great for them, or they may be only so-so on participating in what someone has planned but expect to be convinced as they go along.

Gina was in a new mother-daughter book club whose girls were in fifth grade when they got started. After a few meetings, she introduced an idea for a service project that she hoped others would be as excited about as she was.

"I was looking for a nice, literacy-themed service project for our girls to get involved with," says Gina, "and I thought doing something over the holidays might be extra special. I knew I had found the ideal organization in First Book."

First Book is a nonprofit organization that purchases new books to give to children in the United States and Canada. A large chapter operates in Gina's hometown of St. Louis, Missouri; she particularly liked its Books for Kids, Books for Keeps program, an online fundraiser that seemed simple to set up.

"First Book provides all the steps for anyone to be able to set up their own web page, so any donor can go online and make a personal donation via credit card, or even cash or check, since you can download and print a donation form to mail in," says Gina. She also liked the fact that a national publisher was planning to match any funds raised during the month of December. "I thought I had found the perfect opportunity not only to have our girls participate in a community service–minded project during the holiday season, but to really make a difference in our earning potential for First Book, with the publisher matching contributions.

"From the start, I simply got a lot of silence, then some grumbling, then full-out complaints from the moms that it was just all too much during the holidays, and that they would not be able to participate," says Gina. "After reassuring the group and canceling the fundraiser for anyone who simply did not want to participate, I let them know I truly felt that having our girls participate in some type of service project is something I would really like to revisit, but at a later time, when the holiday rush isn't a deterrent. I don't think I will try another fundraising effort during the holiday season. Saving a fundraiser for another time—when everyone isn't so stressed—is the way to go."

MAKE VOLUNTEERING AN ANNUAL EVENT

ALMOST EVERYONE I know who volunteers says the same thing: "The more you give, the more you want to give." Many of the mother-daughter book clubs I connected with have volunteered multiple times, or they plan to. Some of them even started when their girls were much younger than I would have thought was a good age for volunteering.

Jack, of the Volunteer Family, says that when you get kids started volunteering when they are young, "you're establishing a basis for a lifelong habit." If you volunteer for the same cause over and over again, you show kids that a commitment can make a noticeable difference over time. If you volunteer at a different place every year, you help them see all the different kinds of need that may exist in your community, or even around the world.

When you volunteer together as a group, you also help your girls to see that spending time helping others is not just a sacrifice of your time and theirs; it's a way you can have fun with each other.

Finding Volunteer Opportunities Near You

Opportunities to volunteer abound, no matter how old your girls are or what causes they support. To help you find one that's right for your group, check out these resources:

- Points of Light Institute (www.pointsoflight.org): Matches volunteers to projects through its initiative on the Internet, 1-800-Volunteer.org.

- The Volunteer Family (www.thevolunteerfamily.org/ Volunteers): Started by Heather Jack in 2003, after she had difficulty finding projects she could volunteer for with her family. Based in Massachusetts, the website can match families with local volunteer opportunities in forty states.

- VolunteerMatch (www.volunteermatch.org): Launched as an online nonprofit in 1994 to promote community involvement. It also offers frequent webinars featuring tips on how to be a great volunteer.

- Idealist.org (www.idealist.org): Idealist is a project of Action Without Borders, a nonprofit organization founded in 1995, with offices in New York City and Portland, Oregon. Idealist is an interactive site where people and organizations can exchange resources and ideas, and search for volunteer opportunities abroad.

- United Way (www.liveunited.org): One of the better-known nonprofits serving community organizations of all types, United Way has a national network of nearly 1,300 agencies. While you may be familiar with giving to United Way through payroll deductions at work,

▶

▶

you may not know that you can also visit the national website listed above to find opportunities to volunteer at agencies the United Way supports. To find information about your local division, visit the site and type in your zip code.

In most cases, finding a volunteer opportunity through one of these organizations is as simple as plugging in your zip code and specifying the type of issue you would like to address (children and youth; disaster relief; environment; poverty and hunger). You'll get a list of local organizations searching for volunteers.

By doing a little research, you should also be able to find other local organizations operating in your area that are not signed up with a national network. Plug the words "nonprofit organizations in [insert your hometown and state]" into an Internet search engine; then peruse the results. In Portland, Oregon, where I live, the search brings up nonprofit, Yellow Pages–type listings on a site called Portland.Citysearch.com. From there, I can look for agencies that will fit the interests of the moms and daughters in my book clubs, and see what volunteer opportunities they're offering.

Don't forget to tell others you know about your search for a volunteer opportunity as well. You may be surprised by the causes and organizations you discover because someone you know already volunteers for them.

16
SPEND A WEEKEND AWAY

" My daughter Rachel is thirteen years old, and she often com-
pletes the assigned book in a day or so. I, on the other hand,
am the slow, put-it-down-when-I-lose-interest-for-a-while
type of reader. I find myself going to her to say, 'I just read
the part where the baby was kidnapped and then they found
her left in the Baptist church's Nativity scene,' and she'll reply,
'Oh, you're only that far?! Keep reading, Mom. You haven't gotten to the good part yet!' (She says this quite sarcastically, I
might add!)

" The difference in us as readers is a fair reflection of our differences in personalities. The love of reading provides a common bond between us as mother and daughter and helps me
to enjoy my daughter for who she is—the kid who will stay up
past her bedtime just to finish 'one more page, Mom!'"

—Heather Yano
LEDYARD, CONNECTICUT

BONDING ON THE ROAD

WHEN MY BOOK club with Madeleine had been meeting
for about four years, we decided we wanted to spend
a weekend away together. It was easy to plan because Karen
offered to let us stay at her vacation house, which perched on a

beautiful site overlooking a nearby river. All we had to do was pick a date and sign up to cook a meal. When our weekend away arrived, Madeleine and I carpooled to Karen's place with Jayne and her daughter Elisabeth. The fun started as soon as we left the house, with Jayne cranking up old tunes on the car stereo and all of us singing along loudly. Before we knew it, we were pulling into Karen's driveway, where we found Karen and Janelle already relaxing on the deck. Soon the girls were swimming in the river below while the moms watched from the deck above.

Over the next two days we played games, ate pizza for dinner, watched a few movies on TV, chatted late into the night, slept in, and finished off Sunday morning with a leisurely breakfast. By the time we headed home, we had all had such a great weekend that we couldn't wait to go away together again in a year.

WHY GO AWAY WITH YOUR GROUP?

THERE'S NO BETTER way to get closer to the moms and daughters in your group than to spend a weekend together. When you travel away for one or two nights, you can leave distractions behind and really get to know one another. Even if your group is already close, chances are you have very little opportunity to catch up with each other's hectic lives when you are at book club meetings. You're probably too busy eating, talking about the book you've all read, and discussing your next selection.

Another big benefit is that you'll also likely find a few quiet moments to talk to your own daughter. When Madeleine and I traveled to the Oregon coast for a weekend with our book club, she had a driver's permit and needed practice behind the wheel. During the four hours it took us to drive to the beach and back, we had each other's total attention. It was a great time to talk about school and her friends and her thoughts about college, without either of us being distracted by a phone call or an email or any other disruptions.

HOW WILL YOU KNOW YOU'RE READY?

THERE IS NO magic number of years your group should meet before you start packing your suitcases. Whether you're ready for a trip together really depends on the group's dynamics, the ability of all the members to get away, and your agreement about what "fun" means during your time together. In both of my mother-daughter book clubs, we planned our first trip after we had been meeting for four years. By then we all knew each other fairly well, and we couldn't wait to leave our normal responsibilities behind to head out for two days of fun.

Kate's book club was ready to go much sooner. From the beginning, the girls in the group were best friends, so they all felt comfortable being together. They went away for the weekend at the beginning of their second year as a mother-daughter book club, to a vacation home Kate's parents owned that had enough room to fit the entire group.

PLANNING A TRIP THAT WORKS FOR YOU

Y OU MIGHT FEEL intimidated by the thought of planning a trip for a group of ten or twelve or more. But if you talk about expectations ahead of time, then divide tasks among everyone in your club, the project becomes much more manageable. Here are some points to consider.

- **CHOOSING A TIME THAT WORKS:** Your biggest challenge may be finding a weekend that fits everyone's schedule. Talk about the ideal month or months when you'd like to go away; then check calendars four to six months in advance. If members of your group have weekend sports games or art classes or piano lessons that may be difficult to work around, look for Fridays or Mondays off of school so you can combine a Friday/Saturday or Sunday/Monday to schedule your getaway. You may also have to decide if you're willing to go with a majority of the group, instead of 100 percent, if finding a time when everyone is available is too difficult.

- **DISCUSSING A BUDGET:** Everyone probably has a budget in mind, and talking about it up front will help you avoid awkwardness later when you announce you've found the perfect place and the cost is prohibitive to some members in your group. When Catherine and I spent the weekend at the beach with her book club, we spent $50 per night for lodging for each mother-daughter pair. We were also each responsible for a meal that cost about another $50. That added up to $150 for the two nights, not counting transportation and other activities. Whatever you decide on, be sure you have buy-in from all members before you start talking about where you'll stay.

- **DECIDING WHERE TO GO:** Do you long to go shopping together and schedule massages at a spa? Would you rather take long walks on the beach or hike on wilderness trails? Or are you perfectly content to spend a weekend inside, sleeping late and sipping tea on the couch while watching a movie? On one of my weekends away with Madeleine's group, we combined urban and wilderness experiences by scheduling time at a spa one day and hiking alongside a rippling river the next. Picking the right spot may require some compromise, particularly when you factor budget into the equation. But if some in your group absolutely want to avoid urban settings or the outdoors, it's best to find that out before you spend time looking for accommodations.

- **DIVIDING THE TASKS:** In the unlikely event that someone in your mother-daughter book club steps forward to enthusiastically plan your whole weekend, you can skip this step. But most of us have too many other obligations to take on planning a large group trip. Ask for volunteers to research lodging, be in charge of meal sign-up, and suggest activities in the area where you'll be staying. If you sign up for a task that ends up being more work than you anticipated, don't be afraid to ask for help.

- **FINDING A PLACE TO STAY:** When I helped plan the weekend away with Catherine's book club, we already knew we wanted to go to the Oregon coast in November, which meant it was likely to be cold and rainy. Our priority was to find a house that was big enough to let us all sleep comfortably without feeling crowded, and that also had plenty of large common spaces so we could pursue different activities even if we were stuck inside. I found a great home through the website Vacation Rentals by Owner (www.vrbo. com) that fit our budget and had four bedrooms, two family rooms, one pool table, two televisions, and a big kitchen. Don't forget to find out how comfortable your group members are with sharing beds. Will the moms sleep with other moms? Do moms prefer sleeping with their daughters? Do the girls all want to sleep in the same room?

Once you know your destination, brainstorm options for places to stay. Does someone in your group have a vacation home that's big enough to accommodate you? Do you know someone who would be willing to let you rent a vacation home at a reduced rate? Other options include:

- □ Hotels: Hotels may be more expensive, but their benefits include maid service and the fact that no one has to cook. On the downside, they are less likely to have a place where everyone can hang out comfortably.

- □ Bed-and-breakfasts: These may be more affordable than hotels but more expensive than private homes. Breakfast is provided, and there's likely to be a central gathering place for playing games.

- □ Private homes for rent: You can choose the size and price range, plus look for extras, like billiards or Ping-Pong, hot tubs, stereos, and televisions.

- □ Campgrounds that rent cabins or tent sites: These are likely to be the least expensive and most rustic. Benefits often include access to hiking trails, campfire rings for making s'mores, and, depending on location, access to city activities like bowling, museums, and movies. On the other hand, campgrounds will be more weather- and season-dependent, and bathrooms and showers are likely to be down a path.

- □ Group lodges available through organizations such as Girl Scouts, Boy Scouts, and Camp Fire Boys and Girls: If you're all Girl Scouts or members of Camp Fire, there should be no problem booking a local lodge; otherwise, check the organizations' policies to see if nonmembers can rent their properties.

- **ORGANIZING MEALS:** Even if you stay at a hotel or a bed-and-breakfast and you won't be cooking, you should talk about expectations for the kind of food that will please most of you, and make reservations at restaurants if you need to. Think about dietary restrictions—if someone in your group is vegetarian or allergic to nuts, be sure you provide options that will satisfy her as well. Another good thing to talk about is alcohol, and whether all members of your group are comfortable with the moms drinking during the weekend.

If you stay at a home with a kitchen, which is what my mother-daughter book clubs have done, you can divide meal responsibilities in one of several different ways.

- ☐ Have everyone sign up for a meal and bring all the ingredients to prepare it. You can ask more than one mom-daughter pair to share the more expensive meals, which are usually dinners.

- ☐ Develop a shopping list together and have everyone take responsibility for bringing specific items. Then everyone cooks every meal together.

- ☐ Combine home-cooked meals with a meal or two out.

- ☐ Don't forget to include your daughters. They can either work with their moms on meal preparation or be responsible for a meal themselves. On our trip with Catherine's group, the girls made Saturday dinner and dessert, sharing cooking and cleanup tasks. While they did have a little help from the moms, they had a lot of fun working together to put dinner on the table.

- **PLANNING WHAT TO DO:** It's a good idea to talk about expectations before you pack your suitcases. Do you really want to spend every minute together, doing nonstop activities? Would some of you prefer a mix of group and individual time? Do you want to schedule a few hours when the moms will participate in one activity while the girls do another? Depending on where you will stay, have someone in the group look into local moviehouses, theater productions, bowling lanes, ice cream parlors, museums, and aquariums. Think just a little bit outside the box, and you may even all sign up for paintball, laser tag, or glow-in-the-dark golf.

Kate's book club mixed group-activities time with alone time. They talked about the book they had read—*The Secret Life of Bees*—went for walks, shopped, cooked, hung out and talked, and read. They all went to a bead store together, where the girls made jewelry. One of the girls in their group had her twelfth birthday during the weekend, so the other girls made her cards, signs, and a crown she wore during a birthday party they held for her.

MAKING IT WORK FOR EVERYONE

KATE'S CLUB KEPT its activities pretty loose and had to allow time for the girls to spend on homework. There wasn't a lot of structure throughout the weekend. Kate's only complaint? "It was short—from Friday afternoon to Sunday morning—due to people's activities that required them to return home," she says. "The trip was a great idea. Everyone got along, it was very relaxing, and no one wanted to go home!" They all had so much fun, they planned right away to make it an annual event.

As you may have gathered, planning a weekend away that leaves everyone clamoring for more relies on two major factors: communication and flexibility. Talk about what you all would like to see happen on your trip, and be willing to compromise on some of the easier issues. If budget is inflexible, say so. If you hate camping and cooking over an open fire, don't wait until you're pitching a tent to make your feelings known. On the other hand, if you have a phobia about getting sand between your toes and everyone else wants to go to the beach, you may be able to be flexible by looking forward to having an hour or two on your own. And if you can't imagine relaxing while having to think about cooking, prepare your portion of a meal in advance and bring it microwave-ready. You'll never meet the needs of 100 percent of your group members. But if you deliver on the majority, you'll be on your way to a successful trip.

Put Away the Books
And Try These Games

If I hadn't gone on weekend trips with my mother-daughter book clubs, I would never have found out that Jan and Julia play a cutthroat game of Scrabble, or that Ellen and Joan are fast learners when it comes to shooting pool. Some of the best times you may have during your mother-daughter book club retreat will probably have nothing to do with reading a book. Yes, you can assign a book in advance and find time over the course of two days together to have a relaxed discussion without the stress of homework and bedtime worries. But don't overlook the insights you'll get into the lives of your book club compatriots when you engage in activities that are totally different from your norm. Check with your moms and daughters to find out their list of favorites. Here are some suggestions to get you started:

- **CHARADES:** Who can resist this classic group game of miming clues? Make it specific to your group by having everyone act out the title to a book you've read. You'll probably also learn how the two generations think differently by watching the clues they give

- **CARD GAMES:** Poker, Gin Rummy, Nerts (or Nerk, as we say in my house), Crazy Eights . . . the possibilities are endless. If you don't have favorites of your own, search for websites that will teach you the rules and requirements.

- **SCRABBLE:** While only four people can play officially, any number can look over players' shoulders and help out. Keep a dictionary handy.

▶

- **BOGGLE:** Another great word game. You'll be surprised at how each player turns the jumbled letters into words that she sees easily when others overlook them.

- **APPLES TO APPLES:** This creative wordplay game is fit for a crowd, as it takes up to ten players.

- **PING-PONG, BILLIARDS, DARTS:** If you stay at a private home or bed-and-breakfast featuring any of these games, they can be good for hours of fun and conversation among rotating players.

Part 3

GETTING OVER THE BUMPS: HOW TO HANDLE TYPICAL CLUB CHALLENGES

17

TALKING ABOUT SEX, ALCOHOL, AND OTHER TOUCHY SUBJECTS

> **"** I love being in a mother-daughter book club as a chance to spend some quality time with my daughter both during and outside of the meetings (we read the books out loud together). I also love getting to see the girls grow and change over the years, and I enjoy the social interactions with both mothers and daughters in our group. **"**
>
> —Kate Levin
> NEW YORK, NEW YORK

FROM FANTASY TO REALITY

WHEN MADELEINE'S BOOK club first started, we read a lot of fantasy books and historical fiction. *Dealing with Dragons,* by Patricia Wrede; *Ella Enchanted,* by Gail Carson Levine; *Our Only May Amelia,* by Jennifer Holm; and *The Secret Garden,* by Frances Hodgson Burnett, were some of our favorites. They were sweet books containing lessons about life that were just about right for nine- and ten-year-old girls. They were also comfortable books for us moms to read and discuss with our daughters.

As the girls got older, the books got edgier. *Angus, Thongs and Full-Frontal Snogging,* by Louise Rennison, let us talk about being attracted to boys and kissing them. *Tangerine,* by Edward Bloor, brought up the subject of bullying and social acceptance, and Angela Johnson's *The First Part Last* dealt with a single teenage father raising his child. But when the girls were thirteen, one of them suggested reading *Speak,* by Laurie Halse Anderson. That's when one of our moms put the brakes on—*Speak* deals with date rape and its consequences, and she didn't think we were ready to talk about that yet.

Regardless of whether the moms were ready to bring sex so openly into our discussions, we got the message from the girls that *they* were. They were just finishing eighth grade and on the verge of entering high school. They were worried about how their lives would change, and they wanted to read a book about other teens dealing with issues they might have to face themselves.

After much discussion, the moms decided we should go ahead and read *Speak,* and we were glad we did. When we met to talk about the book, the girls brought up issues that were worrying them. Reading the book opened up an avenue of dialogue about many topics that are hard to bring up out of the blue.

WHY TALK ABOUT SEX, ALCOHOL, AND DRUGS AT ALL?

IF YOU FIND yourself clinging to the fantasy books in your mother-daughter book club, you may be wondering why you would ever want to stray away from those safe titles and choose something that might make any of your members feel uncomfortable.

As president of the Minneapolis-based Search Institute, one of the country's largest research centers on positive youth development, and author of *Sparks: How Parents Can Ignite the Hidden Strengths of Teenagers,* Peter L. Benson, PhD, focuses on ways to connect with teens on many issues. He says there are several reasons for initiating open discussions about sex, drugs, and alcohol.

"In my experience with sex and drug education, it is critical that adults share and be clear about their point of view on these topics, but they need to communicate in a way that young people will be receptive to hear," says Benson. "I think teenagers want to know how adults process the information they are going through. That way they can see the social norms that exist in the world and in that room [where moms and daughters are meeting]."

Benson says he sees mother-daughter book clubs as the reincarnation of the "circle of elders," the new campfire, where "elders gather to impart the wisdom they have learned in a non-threatening way. It is powerful to have dialogue in a circle of intergenerational people."

If you look through this lens, you can begin to see the importance of reading books with your daughter that address some of these tough topics. Etta Gold, who, as head librarian of Temple Beth Am, near Miami, Florida, leads three mother-daughter book clubs, agrees that it's crucial for moms and daughters to talk about these issues together.

"Mother-daughter book clubs provide a safe environment where no one's going to really holler and scream at each other (too embarrassing)," says Gold. "When several teens are talking in a relaxed and uninhibited manner with several mothers, girls can gauge their mothers' reactions to what someone else says, and mothers can be made aware of daughters' concerns by way of others' remarks. There is power and support in numbers— not that they necessarily line up with all the mothers on one side and all the girls on the other."

HOW WILL I KNOW IT'S THE RIGHT TIME TO READ A BOOK ABOUT ONE OF THESE TOPICS?

DECIDING WHEN YOUR daughters are ready to tackle more mature subjects can be tricky. You don't want to push them into age-inappropriate material, yet you don't want to hold them back when they are ready to learn more, either. In some respects, you can let the girls be your guide: You can expect your daughters to hear about what other girls are reading, and to know the issues those books address, so if they ask to read a book that touches on a hot topic, you should consider the request, even if you think it's too early to talk about the questions the book brings up.

Lindsay Kahoe, a librarian at the Carmel Clay Public Library in Carmel, Indiana, says that if a mom or a girl asks for a book that is too mature for some members of the group, she looks for a title that covers the same topic but in a more age-appropriate way. This is always an option for your group.

You may also consider scheduling reading the book some-time down the road. When girls in Mindy's book club asked to read *The Sisterhood of the Traveling Pants,* by Ann Brashares, the moms knew one of the characters in the book decides to have sex, and they thought their girls were too young for that discussion. A couple of years later, the movie was about to come out and the girls really wanted to see it. At that point, the moms agreed to read the book and see the movie as a group.

"We told them that we would all read the book, talk about it as moms and daughters, and then talk about it again as a group. It was one of our more memorable meetings, because they all read it and had lots to say about it," says Mindy.

I'M AFRAID I'LL BE TOO EMBARRASSED

SOMETIMES YOU MAY hold back from talking about sex because you are afraid you will be embarrassed to talk in a group about this topic. You may also be worried that talking about sexual activity or other high-risk behaviors, such as drinking or using drugs, could mislead your daughter to think you condone these behaviors.

Nathalie Bartle knows what you may be feeling. Bartle is the author of *Venus in Blue Jeans: Why Mothers and Daughters Need to Talk About Sex* and a professor at Drexel University School of Public Health, in Philadelphia, Pennsylvania. She has spent much of her career talking to teens and their parents about sex.

"Embarrassment? Yes! My face will get red at times, and I've been talking about these things for years and years," says

Bartle. "I think a mother can say, 'This embarrasses me, too,' but then go ahead and talk about it."

Bartle also has advice for moms who are concerned that talking about sex or other touchy subjects with their daughters may seem to condone behavior the mothers don't actually approve of. "There is no scientific literature to support the belief that talking about these issues with your kids will lead them to becoming sexually active at an earlier age or becoming promiscuous," she says. "In fact, it goes the other way. Your kids are less likely to be sexually active if they can talk to you about their concerns."

I DON'T WANT TO ANSWER QUESTIONS ABOUT WHAT I DID WHEN I WAS THEIR AGE

WHAT IF YOU'RE concerned that your daughter will want to know about your past behavior, and you don't want to share it? In Bartle's opinion, "you don't have to lay it all out in terms of everything you have done, but at the same time, I think you can have a little more honest discussion. You may want to say, 'I did this and I really wish I hadn't. I think I learned something from that, and I would hope you would make a different decision.'"

Benson agrees with this approach. He says that "sexual decisions are complicated. They're about the moment, a week from now, a month from now, and years from now. When you tell stories about what happened after a decision was made, it helps kids see there are consequences to taking certain paths."

Be careful, though, not to preach. If you say something like, "I did this and it was a mistake, so I'm going to make sure you won't make the same mistake," your teen may just shut down and tune you out. When you reveal personal information about your own behavior to your daughter without making a value judgment about how she should behave, you show her that you trust her, and you increase the likelihood of her hearing what you have to say.

Benson reiterates that he believes kids are accumulating information and looking for authenticity. "Young people develop morals and values by gathering in wisdom and having quiet time to reflect upon what they have taken in," he says.

The bottom line is to decide what you're comfortable sharing, keep it relevant to the topic and the girls' age, and not be afraid to open up a bit.

INITIATING DIALOGUE BY TALKING ABOUT CHARACTERS IN A BOOK

YOU MAY FIND It easier to talk about many different issues in a mother-daughter book club than you would talking about them alone with your daughter. That's partly because you are not bringing up the subject to discuss her individual behavior or her friends' actions; you are talking about characters in a book. Gold, of Temple Beth Am, agrees: "Our discussions invariably lead to questions like 'What do you think that character should or could have done differently?' or 'Did that person do anything you didn't like? When the character did that, did you like them less? Did you want to warn that character not to be foolish?' By answering these questions honestly and directly, everyone speaks her own mind," says Gold.

We had the same success in my book club with my daughter Catherine when the girls were thirteen and we read *Amazing Grace,* by Megan Shull. Grace, the main character, goes out to a party and drinks too much. When she is drunk, she has trouble assessing her own safety, and she almost gets hurt. When it came time to discuss the book, the girls talked about how Megan had put herself at risk, and how she did not make good decisions. They all said they wanted to warn her not to do what she was doing. By focusing our conversation on the character, we could freely talk about behavior that was inappropriate for teen girls without preaching or raising their defenses.

MOMS BENEFIT FROM DISCUSSIONS, TOO

I<small>T'S NOT JUST</small> the daughters who benefit from hearing what their mothers have to say about a broad range of social and moral issues—you can benefit from open discussions as well. In Marci's book club, she says the girls tend to open up about the subjects that have come up in books, and that helps her get to know her daughter better.

"I don't know if the girls forget that the moms are there and speak freely, like they would with their friends alone, or if they are grateful for the umbrella of safety and support that the moms bring, but it hasn't seemed to stifle the conversations at all having everyone together. It is invaluable to me to have this insight into my daughter's life outside the home and hear her articulate with her group things that she may feel uncomfort-able talking about with me," says Marci.

Other Resources To Help You Learn About Your Growing Daughter

As your daughter grows and matures, many issues may arise that send you seeking information from experts. Here's a list of parenting books that may be good resources for answering questions on child development and parenting.

- *Ages and Stages: A Parent's Guide to Normal Childhood Development,* by Charles E. Schaefer and Theresa Foy DiGeronimo. This guide discusses five areas of a child's psychological health—emotional, cognitive, friend-ship/relationships, personal growth, and morality—from birth to age ten.

- *The Care and Keeping of You: The Body Book for Girls,* by Valorie Schaefer: Published by American Girl Library, this book can answer just about any question a girl, or her mom, has about her body and her emotions.

- *Childhood Unbound: Saving Our Kids' Best Selves— Confident Parenting in a World of Change,* by Ron Taffel: Taffel offers parents fresh ideas to help guide their children through their teens, including sugges-tions for getting their attention, setting reasonable limits, and engaging them in conversation.

- *The Mother of All Parenting Books: The Ultimate Guide to Raising a Happy, Healthy Child from Preschool*

▶

through the Preteens, by Ann Douglas: Addressing health and parenting issues about your children as preschoolers through preteens, this guide covers a wide variety of topics, including sibling rivalry, bullying, and discipline.

- *Nurture the Nature: Understanding and Supporting Your Child's Unique Core Personality,* by Michael Gurian: From the author of *The Wonder of Boys* and *The Wonder of Girls,* this book encourages parents to trust their own instincts in parenting, based on the core personalities of their children.

- *Parenting by Heart: How To Stay Connected to Your Child in a Disconnected World,* by Ron Taffel and Melinda Blau: Based on a series of workshops, this book debunks parenting myths and outlines different ages that require different styles of parenting.

- *Parenting Preteens with a Purpose: Navigating the Middle Years,* by Kate Thomsen: This practical guide can help parents handle many issues that arise before their children become teens, including bullying, body image, peer pressure, and eating habits.

- *Sparks: How Parents Can Ignite the Hidden Strengths of Teenagers,* by Peter L. Benson, PhD: This guide helps parents determine how they can champion a teen's development from the inside out, helping him or her thrive and become an engaged, successful adult.

- *Uncommon Sense for Parents with Teenagers,* by Michael Riera: Written by a school counselor, this

book provides practical advice to help parents understand their teens.

- *Venus in Blue Jeans,* by Nathalie Bartle and Susan
Lieberman: The authors cover the importance of talking about sexuality with your daughter, as well as
ideas about how to have those discussions.

18
SOLVING CONFLICTS WITH OTHER MEMBERS

" We are equal members discussing wonderful literature, and at the same time we're opening a dialogue with our daughters that will last a lifetime. "

—Sheila Ferry
BELLEVUE, WASHINGTON

CAN YOU AVOID CONFLICT?

YOU PROBABLY HOPE you never encounter conflict of any kind in your mother-daughter book club. Yet if your group is fortunate enough to continue meeting for a number of years, there is almost no way to avoid it altogether. The larger your group, the greater the chance you will come across an issue that pits members against each other, although small groups are not exempt from conflict by any means.

Conflict may arise over many topics:

- The type of books being chosen: As I pointed out in the last chapter, daughters may be ready to tackle books with mature themes before moms are. Moms in your group may also be divided over what kinds of books are acceptable, with some being more lenient and others more conservative.

- Differences of opinion among members about issues raised in a book: Politics, religion, sex . . . all the subjects you are warned to avoid in polite conversation will probably come up at some point in your discussions. Disagreements on any of those topics can bloom into conflict.

- Moms or daughters consistently not reading book selections: Life circumstances may intervene occasionally to prevent you from reading a book, but if someone routinely doesn't read and participate in conversation, it can be frustrating for everyone else in the group.

- Daughters frequently attending without their moms, and vice versa: Again, if a mom occasionally sends her daughter with someone else or comes without her daughter, it probably won't be an issue, but if a mom or daughter often shows up alone, it may point to a lack of commitment that disrupts the group.

- Events unrelated to book club that happen to the girls at school: Disagreements in other venues, like school or Girl Scouts, can spill over into your meetings. Maybe one of the girls was not invited to a birthday party and the others were, or one girl is feeling ostracized at lunch or on the playground.

- Someone in the group regularly monopolizes discussion time: This is more likely to cause frustration than outright conflict, but it could escalate into a bigger issue.

- Events that happen between moms and daughters unrelated to book club: When moms and daughters are at odds over issues at home, the strain sometimes carries over into book club discussions—and that conflict might boil over when you are talking about a particular character's actions. For instance, if the girl character in your book goes against her mother's wishes by wearing clothes the mom doesn't approve of, discussing it may provoke nasty comments between a mother and daughter who are experiencing the same situation at home.

CONFLICT CAN BE A GOOD THING

WHEN MEMBERS OF your mother-daughter book club disagree, your first instinct may be to clam up and pretend it isn't happening. You almost certainly will have a difficult time seeing the disagreement in a positive light. Yet Catherine Weigel Foy, the clinical lecturer and therapist with the Family Institute at Northwestern University who was mentioned in Chapter 2, says that conflict can be quite positive.

"If daughters can learn that having conflict doesn't mean that the relationship is over, they have learned a very important skill in life," says Foy. "If the conflict is kept at a manageable level where it's not inconsistently or unpredictably escalating, then it can be healthy, and differences can be talked about in a very significant way. If girls learn that skill with their moms, then they are more likely to be able to use it in adolescence with their peers. That's where I see conflict as healthy."

KEEP CONFLICT FROM ESCALATING

FOY TEACHES MOMS and daughters to recognize when they're heading to what she calls "the point of no return." "I help them learn to monitor themselves physically as their heartbeat is beginning to raise or they feel flushed," she says. "When they feel in their body that things are escalating, they can take that as a sign to say, 'I need a break.' I advise them not to say what they want to say at that moment, because it could escalate the situation." Tapping into the concept of taking a time-out, Foy recommends that when a mom or a daughter starts to feel this way, she can say, "Excuse me for a moment. I'm going to get a glass of water." But she stresses that it's important to revisit the issue and talk about it when you are ready to see more than just an angry perspective.

LOOK TO A FACILITATOR

KATIE O'DELL, THE school-age services manager at Multnomah County Library in Portland, has had years of experience facilitating book groups. She believes it's easier to deal with conflict if someone is in charge of the meeting, whether that person is a regular facilitator or the hosting mom. "The facilitator can remind the members that the group has gathered together to discuss books and the ideas presented in them," she says, and can tell the group, "If the discussion can return to the book, we can avoid serious conflict."

Etta Gold, the librarian for Temple Beth Am, near Miami, who leads several mother-daughter book clubs, also says that the facilitator can really set the stage by creating an atmosphere of warmth, confidentiality, and solution-oriented answers. Gold says she is always ready to jump in with a diversionary tactic when conflict threatens. She might throw out a question to change the subject, or gently interrupt someone who is talking too much and move the discussion on to a new topic.

MANAGING CONFLICT THAT SIMMERS, NOT ERUPTS

NOT ALL CONFLICTS that your group faces will boil over during a meeting. Some ongoing issues may be frustrating for group members, but they don't know how to address them. If the conflict is between two moms or two daughters, it's probably best for the two members to meet privately to talk about any issues. For instance, if you gently remind a mom that she agreed to attend book club consistently with her daughter when she joined the group, and tell her that you think her daughter feels uncomfortable being at meetings often without her, it may be just the prompt she needs to make book club a priority.

In fact, referring back to your ground rules (see the sample in Chapter 6) could be the simplest way to bring up a topic that's bothering you. What if you didn't set ground rules when you started? In that case, O'Dell says, it's okay to set them even if your group has long been established. In that case, you may want to bring it up when the group is all together. You could say something like, "I know we didn't set any ground rules when we got started two years ago, but I feel it would be helpful if we all agreed to some basic guidelines that will help our group be consistent. Can we talk about that?"

DOS AND DON'TS FOR RESOLVING CONFLICT

MOST EVERYONE OVER the age of three recognizes that throwing a tantrum when you are upset is not the most effective way to resolve conflict. But remaining calm to effectively communicate about an issue may not be easy for you at any age. Here's a list of things that are likely to be helpful, followed by a list of actions you should avoid when you are working through an issue with someone in your book club.

Do:

- Listen to the opposing point of view without interrupting. Clear your head of everything you want to say, and really listen to the other person as she speaks. Focus on her words, not on your emotions.

- Be respectful. Calling names, denigrating another's ideas, or using dismissive body language signals that you have no intention of working out the issue. Also, resist making a statement like, "You are so close-minded." An accusation will usually shut down any attempt to resolve conflict.

- Focus on expressing your feelings and explaining your reasons for your stance. Say something like, "I am worried that if we read this book, our daughters won't understand how to deal with the issues it brings up."

- Let the other person know that you empathize with how she feels. Say something like, "I had not thought of it that way," or, "I can see why that may be upsetting to you."

- Brainstorm solutions. For instance, if there is conflict in your group because someone routinely doesn't read the book, you could suggest that she listen to it on audiotape, or that she turn reading into a mother-daughter activity. Remind her that you are looking for solutions because you really value hearing her thoughts during group discussions.

Don't:

- Ignore the issue. While you may need time to communicate exactly what you want to say, don't wait so long that it seems awkward to bring it up again. You may be lulled into thinking that the conflict has simply gone away, when in fact it's still smoldering just below the surface. It's better to deal with it openly than to wait for something to trigger it again.

- Allow moms to jump in and resolve the issue for girls; instead, they should help the girls figure out how to address what's bothering them directly and how to resolve issues on their own. This will help the girls work through difficult situations whenever adults are not around to intervene.

- Embarrass a mom or daughter in your group or push her into a corner publicly; doing so may make her feel she has to lash out and resist even more.

- Say, "Yes, but . . . " when listening to someone tell why she's upset. When you immediately refute the other person's point of view, you signal that you are not willing to work on the issue.

SEARCH FOR COMMON GROUND

EVEN WHEN YOU don't agree on the issues, you can look for common ground that may lead to a compromise you can live with. For instance, if one or more of your moms believe your book club is choosing to read books that are too mature for the girls, you may want to focus first on what you agree on. In this case, you may say that you all want what's best for your daughters. Then you can talk about what that means to each of you, using "I" statements such as, "I don't want my daughter to be exposed to concepts she's not old enough to understand," or, "I want my daughter to learn about these situations in a safe environment so we can talk about it together."

THINK ABOUT WHAT YOU HOPE TO ACHIEVE

WHEN YOU ADDRESS conflict in your mother-daughter book clubs, you let your members know that their opinions and their values are important. You want them to feel safe expressing their points of view about real-life issues, as well as about those that appear on the pages of the books you read. If you find yourself at an impasse even after you have discussed effectively what's bothering you, you will have to decide how important the issue is to you. Can you live with the situation the way it is, or do you feel you must leave the group? When you work respectfully at finding a resolution first, you increase the chances of keeping your relationships intact, whatever you decide.

Addressing Conflict through Fiction

Sometimes, reading about the way fictional characters address conflict can help you work through your own real-life issues. Try reading some of these novels to talk about how others deal with disagreements.

CLUBS WITH YOUNGER DAUGHTERS

- *Flipped,* by Wendelin Van Draanen: A girl and a boy find lots to like and dislike about each other.

- *Granny Torrelli Makes Soup,* by Sharon Creech: A wise old Italian granny shares words of wisdom and soup

▶

with her granddaughter, who has a disagreement with her longtime friend and neighbor.

- *The Mother-Daughter Book Club* series, by Heather Vogel Frederick: Disagreements between moms, between daughters, and within the book group abound throughout the series. The characters resolve them and provide good examples of ways to deal with people who annoy you, even when they are your friends.

- *P.S. Longer Letter Later,* by Paula Danziger and Ann M. Martin: Two girls who write to each other after one of them moves away deal with family frustrations and other issues that threaten to end their friendship.

- *Tangerine,* by Edward Bloor: Conflict develops between brothers, students at rival schools, and members of a community, with a surprising twist.

CLUBS WITH OLDER DAUGHTERS

- *The Curse of Addy McMahon,* by Katie Davis: Family conflict and misunderstandings between friends in a graphic novel–ish context.

- *Girlwood,* by Claire Dean: Conflicts between friends, within a family, and among neighbors all erupt when a teen runs away from home and a developer wants to raze the woods where her sister believes she's hiding.

- *North of Beautiful,* by Justina Chen Headley: Characters avoid conflict before learning how to stand up for themselves respectfully.

▶

- *The Sisterhood of the Traveling Pants* series, by Ann Brashares: There's almost nothing the pants can't help these girls overcome, whether they are working through issues amongst themselves, with their parents, or with their friends.

- *Songs for a Teenage Nomad,* by Kim Culbertson: Mother and daughter disagree on how much and what kind of information the daughter is entitled to know about their troubled past.

19
WHAT HAPPENS WHEN SOMEONE WANTS TO QUIT?

" I have most enjoyed observing what catches my daughter's eye in a book and listening to her articulate her view. It is a tangible way to watch your child develop into the person she is becoming by participating in discussions that challenge her thoughts and feelings. "

—Emma Gilleland
PORTLAND, OREGON

NOT PART OF THE PLAN

THE LAST THING on your mind when you create a mother-daughter book club is having someone leave the group. Building your club can be fun and energizing. You're looking toward the future, and it can be hard to imagine how that future will change. But life isn't static, it's dynamic, and the changes that come along will undoubtedly affect your mother-daughter book club in some way.

You may find that some club members leave very quickly, and others after years with your group. Some will be happy to say goodbye, while others will leave only because they have to. Either way, losing members of your group can have a lasting effect on the members who remain, and it's best to take a close look at the reasons they leave so you can make sure your mother-daughter book club is fundamentally strong.

REASONS FOR LEAVING

THERE ARE MANY reasons someone may choose to leave your club, including:

- It wasn't what she expected when she signed up.
- She decides to take up another activity and no longer has time for book club.
- It feels too much like school.
- Her one close friend in the group drops out, and she doesn't feel a particularly strong connection with the other members.
- She consistently disagrees with book choices most others in the group like.
- She has an irresolvable conflict with another member.
- She discovers that she really doesn't like reading very much.

I even read a comment once from a mother who said she and her daughter left their book club because the mother didn't like being told what to read! It made me wonder why she wanted to be in a book club in the first place. And that's part of the point: Some moms and daughters will sign up because it sounds like a fun thing to do and their friends are in the club. Once they start going to meetings, they discover it's not really what they expected, or they don't like it as much as they thought they would. Moms and daughters who are less enamored of your book club may never fully bond with the rest of the group, and may even leave within the first year.

LOSING A MEMBER, KEEPING THE CLUB

IT'S IMPORTANT TO keep in mind that when someone quits, it doesn't have to threaten your entire club. In fact, many moms have told me that when members left, it had just the opposite effect on the remaining moms and girls: They became even more committed to making sure the club thrived. For instance, Lisa's club has experienced lots of fluctuation, with several members coming and going in the first year. "The ones who have stayed for each month's meeting have become closer and more friendly," she says, adding that she believes part of the group's continued success is that it still had enough members to have great discussions. Lisa also thinks it helped that the moms and daughters who left did so shortly after the group formed, before the group had had time to bond.

Denise also feels that the moms and daughters in her group became more committed after others left. "We had some people quit right away," she says. "Then we had a really solid group, until one girl was going to high school—when she left, the girl closest to her in age and her mom dropped out almost immediately. But the girls who are the mainstay of the group are very committed."

TALK ABOUT WHY MEMBERS LEAVE

EVEN IF YOUR remaining club members are strongly devoted to your group, you should probably always talk about why someone left. It may be difficult for you to understand how anyone could choose to leave book club, but you should try to find out if that person left because she was not personally committed, or if it was for a deeper reason that may affect others in your group. Depending on why someone left, ask yourselves a few questions to see if you need to make changes.

For instance, if a mom and her daughter quit because the daughter said book club was too much like school, you could ask:

- Do moms tend to act like teachers, making sure the girls learn a lesson during discussion time?
- Do you schedule enough time for social or fun activities during your meetings?
- Are there too many rules to follow when you get together?

If you lose members because of conflict with others in the group, it's especially important to take a look at the cause. Ask yourselves:

- Could we have done anything to help avoid this conflict?
- Is there any way others in the group could have helped solve the problem?
- What can we do to make sure everyone feels welcome when they're at book club meetings?

If someone leaves because she consistently doesn't like the book choices, you may want to look at how your group chooses books. If the members have wide-ranging reading abilities, you'll have to be extra careful in choosing books that are generally not too easy or too hard for your variety of readers. (Refer back to Chapter 7 for ideas on how to pick titles for your book club.) Also keep in mind that reading for book club should be fun, it should be thought-provoking in some way, and it should give you lots to talk about. By making a little effort, you'll find that choosing books that work most of the time for most people in your club should not be too difficult.

On the other hand, if you lose members who say they have signed up for another activity they really want to dedicate time to, it's probably best not to fret too much. They may be your friends, and you may miss seeing them at meetings. But having moms and daughters who are the most interested in going to book club, even if it means crunching time somewhere else, will probably make your club stronger in the long run.

WHEN SOMEONE MOVES AWAY

SOMETIMES A MOM and daughter leave book club because they have no choice—they are moving to another town or another country. If this happens in your group, you might look at it as an opportunity to schedule some kind of send-off event or bon voyage party. The possibilities are as varied as mother-daughter book clubs themselves.

In Denise's book club, when one of the moms and her daughter moved to England, their book club members wanted to do something special to let them know they would be missed. "We had a 'tea' for them at Panera bakery, which was really nice to our group," says Denise. "They didn't mind if we held book club meetings there, and the girls, especially the girl leaving the group, *loved* their hot chocolate, which they serve in huge ceramic mugs with whipped cream and chocolate syrup. We found a card with red balloons on it [the group's name was Red Balloons], and bought her an address book with contact info for everyone, and a journal. We didn't have any real ceremony, but I talked about how much we would all miss them, and how much they added to the group. The kids all spoke in ridiculously bad English accents. It was a sweet event."

Denise's mother-daughter book club still hears from the mom and daughter who moved away. In fact, the two went to a book signing by Cornelia Funke and got the book club an autographed copy of the author's newest book, which hadn't even been released in the United States yet.

OTHER REASONS FOR LEAVING

THERE ARE OTHER reasons a mom and daughter may leave your club even if they love the group and want to stay.

- If the mom is getting divorced, dealing with the negotiations may sap all her time and energy.
- A mom or daughter may come down with a long-term illness that keeps her away from the group.
- A mom's work schedule may change, making it difficult for her to make it to meetings consistently.

It's hard to know what life changes will occur among all your moms and daughters when you meet as a group for years. But a strongly bonded mother-daughter book club can really provide support to its members who need it, whatever circumstances arise.

First, you can encourage the mom and daughter who are leaving to take a "sabbatical," instead of quitting. It may be hard for them to foresee a time when they will be able to return, but they'll know the door is open for them to come back when and if their lives return to normal. Second, if their family needs assistance with making meals or shopping for groceries or running other errands, your other group members can sign up to help. The bigger the group, the easier it will be for you to chip in and spread out the load to all members. Third, you can send periodic updates or cards to let them know you're thinking of them and will gladly welcome them back when they are ready.

In cases like these, you can still schedule some kind of recognition event to acknowledge your group is changing. It's easier to deal with the sadness you may all feel over what's happening if it's out in the open.

STAYING THE COURSE

SCHEDULING A BON voyage party or some other event to say goodbye is as much for the moms and daughters who stay with your club as it is for the ones who leave. Denise says that was definitely true for her club. "We did it to help the pair that was leaving, but I also think it helped solidify those who were staying as well," she says.

Showing all your book club members that you value them as part of your group is definitely a side benefit of saying goodbye to ones who find they must go.

Gifts for Book Lovers

If you decide to schedule a goodbye party for your book club members who are leaving, you may want to consider exchanging gifts to have a lasting reminder of the event. But you don't have to wait until someone decides to leave your club to celebrate. You can throw a party and have a gift exchange for many reasons, including your book club anniversary or a holiday.

Julie's book club, for example, had been meeting for less than a year when they decided to schedule a gift exchange. "We thought it would be fun to make our holiday book club meeting a little special," says Julie, so they agreed to each bring a wrapped book. Some girls brought new books, while others brought used ones, a suggestion Julie made to help everyone keep costs down. They exchanged presents in what Julie referred to as a Yankee swap: Each girl drew a number, then picked a present in numerical order. Once all the presents were opened, each girl got to say which book she'd brought and why she liked it. Julie says the gift exchange was a lot of fun, and everyone ended up with a "new to her" book.

Check out the suggestions below to find some ordinary and not-so-ordinary gift ideas for book lovers.

BOOK ACCESSORIES

- Bookmarks: Easy to make or to buy, bookmarks can be personalized to match the people who receive them.

- Book lights: For book lovers who have trouble putting pages aside even after everyone else is asleep.

- Book plates: For anyone who collects books to build her personal library, a book plate can help any tome find its way home, even if it's loaned out to friends.

- Book tote: Find one with a favorite quote or the name of your favorite bookstore. Even better, buy a blank tote and personalize it with your favorite literary quote.

BOOKS ON BOOKS

- *Book Lust: Recommended Reading for Every Mood, Moment, and Reason* and *Book Crush: For Kids and Teens—Recommended Reading for Every Mood, Moment, and Interest,* by Nancy Pearl

- *The Ultimate Teen Book Guide,* edited by Daniel Hahn and Leonie Flynn

BOOKS FOR PEOPLE WHO LOVE TO COOK

- *The Mother Daughter Cookbook: Recipes to Nourish Relationships,* by Lynette Rohrer Shirk

- *The Book Lover's Cookbook: Recipes Inspired by Celebrated Works of Literature and the Passages That Feature Them,* by Shaunda Kennedy Wenger and Janet Jensen

BOOK JOURNALS

- *Book Lust Journal,* by Nancy Pearl

- *A Book Lover's Diary,* edited by Shelagh Wallace

- *Books To Check Out: A Journal,* by Imagineering Company

- *Books To Check Out for Kids,* by Imagineering Company

BOXED BOOK SETS

Great for girls or moms who like books in a series or by one author. Some possibilities:

- Gertrude Chandler Warner's *The Boxcar Children* series

- E. B. White's *Charlotte's Web, The Trumpet of the Swan,* and *Stuart Little*

- Ann Brashares' *The Sisterhood of the Traveling Pants* series

- Jane Austen's *Emma, Sense and Sensibility, Pride and Prejudice,* and *Persuasion*

- J. R. R. Tolkien's *The Lord of the Rings* trilogy

- J. K. Rowling's *Harry Potter* series

MAGAZINES ON BOOKS

- *The New York Review of Books*

- *Bookmarks*

- *The New York Times Book Review*

- *The Horn Book Magazine*

- *Publisher's Weekly*

GIFT CERTIFICATES

- Gift card to a favorite bookstore: The recipient can pick out her favorite book.

- Gift card to CafePress: The recipient can look for hard-to-find book-related products, like T-shirts, pajamas, and more.

MISCELLANEOUS

- Book-opoly: Who can resist a game whose object is to collect bookstores and trade them for libraries? Property deeds include interesting facts about books and authors.

- Action figures: Get a figurine of a favorite writer, like Jane Austen, William Shakespeare, or Charles Dickens. Or go for every reader's favorite superhero—the librarian.

20
ADDING NEW MEMBERS TO YOUR ESTABLISHED GROUP

" Our mother-daughter book club has been great. I don't usually take the time to read the books my daughter is reading, so for me it was a great way to make sure that I do. We have loved discussing the book club books before, during, and after meetings. It's also nice to have a social gathering of other moms and daughters the same age. We talk about the book, as well as lots of other things on our minds. I also love how our book club comes up with fun, creative ways to heighten the experience. For example, when we met to discuss *Hoot* [by Carl Hiaasen], a naturalist from the forest preserve brought a real, live owl to our meeting! It was very exciting. **"**

—Lisa Bany-Winters
GLENVIEW, ILLINOIS

SETTING OUT THE WELCOME MAT

Your MOTHER-DAUGHTER book club would be unusual if you didn't consider adding new members at some point. Friends hear about how much fun you have at meetings and ask to join. You lose a member or two and decide you need to beef up your ranks by asking new people to sign on. Whatever the reason, accepting new members into your established group will most likely require that both the people already in your book club and the new people joining make an adjustment. You'll want to do what you can to make the transition as smooth as possible.

THE MORE, THE MERRIER

SOME MOTHER-DAUGHTER book clubs decide from the beginning that they are open to anyone who wants to join. Their members may like being in a large group or may feel more comfortable being inclusive. Julie's mother-daughter book club has been open to new members all along; she says the girls in her club have lots of other activities, which leads to moms' and daughters' not being able to attend meetings. That's okay with Julie's group, because it still has quite a few moms and daughters at each meeting to talk about the book. "Plus, girls like inviting their friends and showing them how much fun the meetings are," says Julie, adding that she thinks "it's wonderful to get young girls reading and sharing their thoughts about books."

Even if you are open to anyone and everyone, you probably have a limit on how many total members you will accept. Julie says that if her club gets too big, she thinks it will reconsider the open policy, but she doesn't know how big "too big" would be. As I discussed in Chapter 3, determining a comfortable group size is a decision each club has to make on its own. For some, eight members will be the limit, while others may be comfortable having up to twenty or more in their group.

SEARCHING FOR NEW MEMBERS

THERE MAY ALSO come a time when you actively search for new members, instead of waiting for them to come to you. You may have started with a small number of moms and daughters in your club, or you may have lost a mother-daughter pair or two and want to have more. The first thing you can do is brainstorm as a group to come up with a list of friends you think may be interested. Then you can assign moms and daughters to contact those you want to invite.

Be prepared to be turned down. It may be hard for you to believe, but not everyone wants to be in a mother-daughter book club. Lisa says she is always disappointed when she tries to recruit new members and the moms tell her they don't want to add another activity. For Lisa, it's a no-brainer to incorporate a once-a-month event you can do with your daughter into your schedule, especially because she considers it so important for girls to read outside of school requirements. As a result, she has tried several other ways to recruit new members for her club.

"I posted flyers at the library and in the library schedule," says Lisa, whose group meets at her local public library. "I sent letters to the moms at my daughter's daycare. I emailed teachers, librarians, and principals at grade schools about the club. I have left our bookmarks at churches, with the Girl Scouts, and at the local gymnastics gym."

Lisa's creative, "guerrilla marketing" approach to attracting new recruits has been successful. Of all her tactics for getting the word out about her club, she says the most effective has been posting notices at the library; that may be because the people who see the notices are more likely to be avid readers. For Lisa, the key was testing out different methods of spreading the message; you can find the one that works best for you by experimenting on your own.

WELCOMING FORMER MEMBERS

DON'T BE SURPRISED if a mom and daughter who quit your club years ago ask to rejoin at some point, especially if they liked being part of your club but quit because of too many other obligations. This happened in my mother-daughter book club with my oldest daughter, Madeleine. Jan and Julia were part of our group for less than a year when they stopped coming to meetings. The only ones they knew in our club at the time were Karen and Kirsten, and the rest of us didn't have much of an opportunity to get to know them well before they left.

When the girls started high school, Jan and Julia asked if they could rejoin our club. By that time, Julia had been in classes with many of the girls in middle school, so she knew several of them better than she had when they were younger and in different elementary schools. While schedules for both mom and daughter were still busy, they wanted to make a commitment to book club. Our group had held steady at five mother-daughter pairs after Jan and Julia left the club, and even though we had bonded tightly during the years they were gone, we were thrilled when they asked to come back.

EASING THE TRANSITION

ANYTIME YOU WELCOME new members, you change the dynamics of your group. Each person will bring her own style and personality to your club, and you should be prepared to accommodate those attributes. The transition will likely be easier if you are used to adjusting to new moms and daughters on a regular basis. The more socially fluid the members in your group are, the better equipped you'll be to make the first few meetings comfortable for moms and daughters who join later.

Audrey and her daughter Lauren were asked to join Lisa's group after the club had been meeting for a few years. Lauren knew most of the other girls in the group, because they all went to the same middle school. Audrey says the invitation to join came at the right time for her and her daughter.

"I was especially excited because my daughter was just becoming an active reader, and this group of girls really increased her interest," says Audrey. "They not only meet once a month, but they often share books throughout the month."

Audrey says both she and Lauren felt well accepted when they first went to meetings. "My daughter is generally a little shy until she gets to know people, so she was quiet for most of the first meeting. I think having a little social time before the meeting actually helped to break the ice."

Jan's advice, after rejoining our club, is to make sure the girls have something in common, and to be certain that the girls in the existing group truly want a new member in their circle. "Adults are generally socially skilled enough to engage a new person in the group. It's tougher for the girl, and it's not going to be a successful integration unless the new girl feels welcomed," says Jan.

"Both Julia and I have felt very welcome, but it wouldn't have worked if Julia didn't know a couple of girls fairly well already and have interests in common with them."

A LOW-KEY FIRST MEETING, VERSUS ONE WITH FANFARE

THE FIRST MEETING Audrey and Lauren attended was just like any other for the mother-daughter book club. There was no big welcoming party or other recognition, and that fit the two of them just fine. "Too much information can sometimes be intimidating," says Audrey. "We had never been in a book club before, so we had no predefined expectations. Just reading the book and attending worked well for us." Audrey says she and Lauren both love their mother-daughter book club, and she's not sure the group could have done anything more to make their entry smooth.

Jan and Julia's transition back into our club was also fairly low-key. After our current members agreed we were happy to have them rejoin, they came to the next meeting and we integrated them into our normal activities. Even though some of us were concerned that they might not feel comfortable speaking up in group discussions at the beginning, we were pleasantly surprised that they jumped into the conversation right away.

Don't settle for the subtle approach, however, if you feel the occasion is a milestone you want to recognize. A younger girl in particular may appreciate fanfare and feel more welcome if her first meeting is also a special event for the whole group. Before the new members attend their first meeting, brainstorm about ways to extend an official welcome. You might put up balloons and play some of the get-to-know-you games mentioned in Chapter 6. Or have everyone work on a card to sign and present when the new members arrive, and then serve cake and ice cream to celebrate the new addition to your group. With just a little planning, you can turn the occasion into something for everyone to remember.

Saying No Is an Option

There's an enormous amount of pressure to say yes when someone asks if she can join your mother-daughter book club. The mom or daughter asking may be part of your social circle. She may be someone you really like and think would be an asset to the group. You may want to avoid being labeled exclusive, as I discussed in Chapter 4. You may even be inclined to offer an invitation on the spot when someone asks. Don't do it, unless you already know that your club is open to all who want to join.

If your group hasn't discussed adding new members, this is an issue you will want to bring up at a meeting. The most important opinions to take into consideration will always be the ones of the moms and girls already in your club. Keep in mind that while you may feel pressured to say yes, there are valid reasons for saying no.

Why would you say no to new members?

- You like the size of your club and don't want it to grow any larger.

▶

▶

- You have bonded tightly as a group and don't want to add new personalities to the mix.

- The new member lives far away, and you want your club members close together so it's easier for everyone to get to meetings.

It's best to decide whether your club is open to new members before you're asked. That way, if the answer is no, you can say so right away and explain why to the person. You may be able to avoid hurt feelings if it's clear the answer is not meant as a personal insult.

Keep in mind that avoiding hurt feelings altogether may not be possible, so be prepared to face them honestly. When a neighbor asked Show-Ling's group if she and her daughter could join their club, the group decided to say no. The book club moms and daughters talked about it at a meeting and decided they really wanted to keep their group just as it was. They were already experiencing difficulty choosing times for meetings, and they didn't want to add another pair of schedules to the mix. They had also bonded really well as a group already.

Their reasons were valid, and when Show-Ling broke the news to the mom who asked to join, she encouraged her to start her own mother-daughter book club. Yet Show-Ling says it wasn't easy turning her down. "It was awkward for a while after that in social occasions when we ran into each other," she says. "I could sense that she wasn't very friendly toward me. It's never easy to say no to someone. In the end, though, I think we made the right decision of sticking with a smaller group."

21
WHEN TO CONSIDER RESTRUCTURING YOUR CLUB

" Although sometimes the books we read bring up subjects that make us uncomfortable or maybe seem too mature for our daughters, we are glad they come up this way—in this safe and open environment where we can share our opinions and hear what our daughters have to say—rather than later, in a typical mother-daughter awkward conversation or, worse, when it's too late. "

—Ellen Calves
GOSHEN, NEW YORK

HITTING CHOPPY WATERS

WHEN MADELEINE AND I had been in our mother-daughter book club for four years, all the moms and daughters went out to a restaurant to celebrate our anniversary. We had a leisurely meal and waited until dessert to talk about the book we had read. We were all so relaxed and having such a great time that we were surprised when one of the girls said she didn't want to be in book club anymore.

Several more girls chimed in to say the same thing, and suddenly we were all paying attention. Our book club, which had been such a treasure for so many years, appeared to be dissolving before our eyes, and we hadn't had a clue that this was coming. The moms listened while several girls told us why they might want to quit:

- They were tired of reading the book for each meeting.

- They thought it would be too difficult to keep up with book club reading once they started high school (they were in eighth grade at the time).

- Some of them didn't want their friends to know they were in a book club with their mothers, because their friends thought it wasn't "cool."

- They thought the moms were not allowing them to choose the kinds of books they wanted to read for book club.

When they were done, we all sat quietly for a moment, trying to decide what to do. No one truly wanted our group to disband, and the girls admitted that they really liked seeing each other regularly. We started to talk about the things we liked about book club. Our social time topped the list, because some of the girls didn't go to the same school. Without book club, they realized they would probably have no reason to see each other at all.

Someone suggested we just stop picking books and continue getting together anyway. But what would a book club be without the books? And some of us were concerned that if we were only a social group, it would be easier to blow off group meetings every month. We kept working through the issues, until we finally settled on a structure that everyone agreed was worth a try.

- We cut back our meetings from once a month during the school year to six times each year. There were six pairs of us in the group, so that meant we would meet at each pair's house once a year.

- We added the possibility of movie discussions to the list. That way, if someone felt we needed a break from reading, she could choose a movie for us to watch and discuss instead.

- We promised more flexibility in book choices. The girls were thirteen and fourteen years old at the time, and they told us they were ready to tackle more mature subjects. We agreed to consider more options.

By the time dinner was over, we were all a little worried about our future as a group but determined to make it work. It's been four years since that night, and our group sailed through the high school years stronger than ever. The changes we made weren't drastic, but they were enough to keep us on track and hold our book club together.

TACKLE THE ISSUES BEFORE THEY TACKLE YOU

IF YOU'RE LIKE most people with complicated lives, once your book club is up and running smoothly, you'll probably never think of making adjustments before the need to do so hits you in the head. Yet if there is one constant in every mother-daughter book club I know of, it is change. That should be expected when you have a variety of people with a lot going on in their lives.

Yet most of us resist change until we can no longer ignore it. If you expect that members of your group will change, too, which probably also means your club will need to change along with them, you're less likely to be blindsided by complaints, like my group was. If your mother-daughter book club is truly important to you, then it's worth it to take the group's temperature every now and then to make sure all is okay.

What are some signs that you may need to regroup and restructure?

- Girls and moms start having more frequent conflicts that make it difficult to schedule meetings.

- Girls and moms who used to talk and contribute to the group no longer put forth the same effort.

- There's consistently no enthusiasm when you announce the book title for your next meeting.

- You go long periods of time without meeting, because the mom and daughter in charge of the next meeting don't set a date or announce a book choice.

GETTING THE FEEDBACK YOU NEED

A GOOD WAY TO make sure your mother-daughter book club stays on track is to build a feedback system into your basic structure. You can do that by making sure you talk openly about what's working and what's not each year, then making adjustments as needed. You can take a survey, like the one suggested in the sidebar for this chapter, and you can create an atmosphere where honest feedback is welcomed. If a girl complains that the books you read are too hard and you dismiss her comments by saying, "I know you're up to the challenge," you're telling everyone that you don't value input.

All of you create your mother-daughter book club every time you get together. So it's best to make sure that all of you are relatively happy with the way you act as a group. I say "relatively" because it's unlikely that 100 percent of you will be happy 100 percent of the time. But if you feel your book club delivers on most of the expectations you have, you will most likely maintain an active, lively group for many years.

And remember to state up front anything you're unwilling to change. Many of the moms in my group balked at omitting a book discussion from our meetings—we felt that it was a primary benefit of being in our group, and we didn't want to give it up completely. We compromised to include movies as well as books, but we were not willing to scrap the discussions altogether.

WHEN TO GET FEEDBACK

YOU CAN BE open to feedback informally all the time, but it's a good idea to make sure you formally ask your group how things are going about once a year. Setting up a planning meeting at the beginning of each school year may be the best time for you: You can talk about the months to come and find out what everyone would like to see continue or change in the year ahead. Or you may want to do it at the end of your book club year, when you have all had a chance to recognize what is and is not working well for your group.

You could also make a group evaluation part of your anniversary celebration, if you have one. In my case, I have one book club that started in February (Madeleine's) and one that started in April (Catherine's). Either month is a good time to check in and see how things are going. February is about the midpoint of our club year, and April is near the end.

Just remember that if you conduct an official survey, you need to make sure you've allowed enough time for people to fill out their answers in advance. Then go over the responses during a discussion scheduled separately from your normal book talk or social time.

STAYING THE COURSE

AFTER THE NEAR disaster my club experienced over dinner those many years ago, we were not sure how things would work out for us, even though we decided on ways to restructure. It was almost like starting over again, except instead of being excited about the times ahead of us, we were apprehensive that our adjustments would not make enough of a difference. As it turned out, not much changed after all, and our group continued to be strong. The most important modifications we made were the ones to meet less often and choose more mature books. Those changes smoothed our girls' transition into high school, and have kept us meeting happily in the years since.

Conduct a Survey

Sometimes the best way to find out what is and isn't working with your group is to conduct a survey. Even if you take informal surveys every now and then by asking your members if they're happy with the way things work in your club, you may not be getting the answers you need to truly know if things are going well. To be sure you get the feedback that's most helpful, you need to:

- Give people time to consider their answers.

- Assure them that no one will know who said what.

You may think it's not important to the moms and daughters in your group to have the option of answering questions anonymously. And you may be right. But everyone will probably appreciate knowing they can answer candidly without worrying about hurting someone's feelings. So take this precaution, even if you feel it is unnecessary.

What's the best way to conduct a survey? First, announce during a meeting that you want everyone's feedback. Then brainstorm a list of questions that you'd like to have answers to. Finally, offer to email the questions so each person can type her answers, print them out, and bring them to the next meeting. If everyone types the answers, there's no handwriting to recognize; plus, it's easier to read the responses quickly.

Here are some questions you may want to ask:

- What do you like most about book club?

- What do you think we could do better?

▶

- Do you think our meetings are too seldom, too often, or just about the right amount of time apart?

- Do you find it difficult to finish reading the book before we meet?

- Do you feel that our book choices are too easy, too hard, or just right?

- Would you like to go on outings as a group?

- If so, suggest places you'd like to go or things you'd like to do together. (Examples are eating at restaurants, going out to movies, going to a bookstore or library, etc.)

- What is your favorite book our group has read?

- What do you wish we did more often?

- Please add any other ideas you have for our group.

Having a combination of open-ended questions and yes-or-no questions keeps the survey easy while enabling you to get more extensive feedback.

You can also combine statements asking members to rate certain issues on a scale of one to five, followed by open-ended questions for others. Here's what that questionnaire might look like:

Rate the following on a scale of one to five. Circle one if you think our club needs a lot of improvement in the area, or five if you think we already do an outstanding job. Three is somewhere in between.

▶

- Our book club meets just about the right number of times each year.
  ① ② ③ ④ ⑤

- I would like to meet less often.
  ① ② ③ ④ ⑤

- I would like to meet more often.
  ① ② ③ ④ ⑤

- The books we read are mostly just about right for me in difficulty.
  ① ② ③ ④ ⑤

- The books we read are too hard for me.
  ① ② ③ ④ ⑤

- The books we read are too easy for me.
  ① ② ③ ④ ⑤

- I would like to move up to more mature subjects.
  ① ② ③ ④ ⑤

- What do you like most about book club?

  _____

  _____

  _____

  _____

- What do you think we could do better?

  _____

  _____

  _____

  _____

▶

▶

- Would you like to go on an outing with the group? If so, where?

  _____
  _____
  _____
  _____

- What is your favorite book our group has read?

  _____
  _____
  _____
  _____

- Is there anything you would like to do at meetings that we don't do now?

  _____
  _____
  _____
  _____

- Is there anything else you think the group should know?

  _____
  _____
  _____
  _____

WHERE TO LOOK FOR BOOKS ON THE WEB

Amazon

www.amazon.com

> Find out what reader reviewers have to say about almost any book in print. Many children's titles feature editorial reviews from School Library Journal, along with age recommendations for the titles.

Barnes & Noble

www.bn.com

> Check B&N Jr. to find books recommended for different age groups, listed by genre.

IndieBound

www.indiebound.org/indie-next-list

> Employees at independent booksellers around the United States make recommendations for each Indie Next List. Lists for kids are published quarterly, and books are divided into categories for readers ages four to eight, ages nine to twelve, and in their teens.

KidsReads.com

www.kidsreads.com

> Part of the Book Report Network, a group of websites founded in 1996. You can expect to find an alphabetical list of reviews, a list of books made into movies, podcasts, and author interviews.

Multnomah County Library, Oregon
www.multcolib.org
> With one of the highest circulations per capita in the country, this public library maintains a list of books and activities for kids and teens. Extras include a family guide to the Internet, and websites where you can find help with homework.

The New York Times Book Review
www.nytimes.com/2009/03/22/books/bestseller/bestchildren
.html?_r=1
> Find current bestsellers for children in chapter books, paperbacks, and series books.

Newbery Medal Home Page
www.ala.org/ala/mgrps/divs/alsc/awardsgrants/bookmedia
/newberymedal/newberymedal.cfm
> This site, courtesy of the American Library Association, provides you with lists of present and past Newbery Medal winners and Honor Books, as well as recipients of several other awards.

Reading Is Fundamental
www.rif.org/educators/books/book_list_index.mspx
> This nonprofit organization dedicated to early literacy has many lists to peruse, including good books for boys, poetry books, and books to adapt into plays. While much of the site is geared toward younger readers, there are also good resources for older kids, teens, and parents.

Reading Rockets
www.readingrockets.org/books/awardwinners#best
> Funded by a grant from the U.S. Department of Education, Reading Rockets is a national multimedia project involving PBS television programs, online services, and professional-development opportunities. On its website, you'll find links to many different book awards, "best of" lists, and other notable-book lists.

TeenReads.com

www.teenreads.com

Another member of the Book Report Network, this site showcases book reviews for teen readers, books to movies, podcasts, author interviews, and other features.

Young Adult Library Services Association

www.ala.org/ala/mgrps/divs/yalsa/booklistsawards/booklistsbook.cfm

This division of the American Library Association maintains lists of best books for young adults, best films, award winners, graphic novels, nonfiction books, and more.

Young Reader's Choice Awards

www.pnla.org/yrca/index.htm

Presented each year by the Pacific Northwest Library Association, Young Reader's Choice Awards nominations are accepted only from children, teachers, parents, and librarians in the Pacific Northwest. Awards are given in three divisions: the junior division, for grades four to six; the middle division, for grades seven to nine; and the senior division, for grades ten to twelve.

ONE HUNDRED BOOKS THAT MIGHT BE RIGHT FOR YOUR BOOK CLUB

HERE'S A LIST of one hundred book titles, grouped by age, that you may want to try in your mother-daughter book club. To see regular updates to the list, check www.mother-daughterbookclub.com.

BOOKS FOR SEVEN- AND EIGHT-YEAR-OLD READERS

1. *Afternoon of the Elves,* by Janet Taylor Lisle: Sarah-Kate is poor, with a sick mother, and is shunned by most of the kids at school. She gets Hillary's help to tend an elf village in her back yard, and the two become friends.

2. *Bed-Knob and Broomstick,* by Mary Norton: The three Wilson children discover that their aunt's prim-and-proper neighbor is actually a witch; she gives them a magical bed-knob they can use to travel through time and space.

3. *Charlie and the Chocolate Factory,* by Roald Dahl: When Charlie wins a ticket to tour Willy Wonka's chocolate factory, he sees an opportunity to bring a little joy into his and his grandfather's lives.

④ *Charlotte's Web,* by E. B. White: An unlikely friendship between Wilbur the pig and Charlotte the spider helps Wilbur become invaluable to his owner.

⑤ *Dealing with Dragons,* by Patricia C. Wrede: A princess defies stereotypical expectations of her position to forge her own way and help her friends when they need her.

⑥ *Eloise,* by Kay Thompson: The classic tale of a girl who lives in New York City's Plaza Hotel with her nanny, her dog, and her turtle.

⑦ *Fairy Dust and the Quest for the Egg,* by Gail Carson Levine: Fans of Tinkerbell and Neverland will enjoy this tale of Prilla, a new fairy in Neverland, who was born of a baby's laugh and must figure out her special talent.

⑧ *Frindle,* by Andrew Clements: When Nick is assigned a report on how entries are added to the dictionary, he is inspired to coin his own new word. His teacher is not amused, and a war about words ensues.

⑨ *From the Mixed-Up Files of Mrs. Basil E. Frankweiler,* by E. L. Konigsburg: When Claudia and Jamie run away and hide in New York City's Metropolitan Museum of Art, they never expect to get involved in an art mystery.

⑩ *Harriet the Spy,* by Louise Fitzhugh: Harriet tries to make sense of everyone around her by spying on them and writing what she sees in a secret notebook. But when classmates ostracize her after reading what she says about them, she must find a way to deal with being an outcast.

⑪ *The Hundred Dresses,* by Eleanor Estes: Schoolmates taunt Wanda Petronski, who wears the same faded dress every day but says she has a hundred dresses at home. When Wanda moves away, Maddie is saddened that she stood by and said nothing while her friends taunted Wanda.

⑫ *Little House on the Prairie,* by Laura Ingalls Wilder: Laura's family moves from their log home in Wisconsin to Kansas Indian country, where they build a little sod house.

13 *The Mouse and the Motorcycle,* by Beverly Cleary: When Ralph Mouse discovers a toy motorcycle, he learns how to ride and makes a new friend in the boy who owns it.

14 *Mrs. Piggle-Wiggle,* by Betty MacDonald: Mrs. Piggle-Wiggle lives in an upside-down house and dispenses wisdom to mothers who come to her seeking innovative cures for common childhood maladies.

15 *Piper Reed: Navy Brat,* by Kimberly Willis Holt: Follow the adventures of Piper, a middle child with a winning voice, and catch a glimpse of the life of a military family.

16 *Pippi Longstocking,* by Astrid Lindgren: After her father's disappearance, Pippi lives all alone, with no one for company but a monkey and a horse. She amazes the neighborhood kids, wants to be a pirate when she grows up, is good at foiling burglars, and is stronger than a circus muscleman.

17 *Premlata and the Festival of Lights,* by Rumer Godden: Premlata is an Indian girl who wants to help her poor family celebrate Diwali, the festival of lights honoring a Hindu goddess.

18 *The Real Thief,* by William Steig: Gawain the goose guards the royal treasury and is fiercely loyal to King Basil. When jewels and other treasures go missing, Gawain is unjustly accused. He escapes and hides out until he can discover the real thief.

19 *Sarah, Plain and Tall,* by Patricia MacLachlan. Sarah leaves her home in Maine to travel to the Midwest in the late 1800s. She is answering an ad from a widowed farmer seeking a wife to care for him and his children after his wife died in childbirth.

20 *The Secret School,* by Avi: When Ida's one-room schoolhouse unexpectedly closes early, the students still want to go to school. Fourteen-year-old Ida secretly takes over as teacher, hoping to earn her way into high school in the fall.

21 *Tales of a Fourth-Grade Nothing,* by Judy Blume: Ten-year-old Peter is a fourth grader trying to figure out how to deal with his little brother, who often gets in trouble while Peter is blamed.

㉒ *The Year of Miss Agnes,* by Kirkpatrick Hill: Miss Agnes arrives on the Alaskan frontier to take over a one-room schoolhouse in 1948. She's different from any teacher the students have ever had, playing opera music, reading books about Greek myths, and even learning sign language so she can teach a deaf student.

㉓ *The Year of the Dog,* by Grace Lin: Grace's parents are from Taiwan, but the family lives in the United States. She must learn to reconcile the culture at home with the culture she sees in school. The book chronicles her journey through the Taiwanese Year of the Dog.

㉔ *The Year the Swallows Came Early,* by Kathryn Fitzmaurice: When Groovy's father is arrested after gambling away the inheritance she had hoped to use to attend cooking school, she must face the betrayal and decide if she can forgive him.

㉕ *Utterly Me, Clarice Bean,* by Lauren Child: When Clarice's best friend, Betty, goes on a trip, Clarice is paired on a project with Karl, the worst boy in class, who turns out not to be so bad after all. When Betty returns, Clarice must patch up a misunderstanding and help prove that Karl has been wrongly accused of stealing.

BOOKS FOR NINE- AND TEN-YEAR-OLD READERS

㉖ *Alphabet of Dreams,* by Susan Fletcher: In ancient Persia, Mitra lives with her younger brother, Babak, in a labyrinth of caves, hiding from their father's enemies and stealing food to survive. Babak has prophetic dreams, and under the guidance of the magus Melchior, his visions lead him and Mitra west as they follow signs in the stars.

㉗ *Anne Frank: The Diary of a Young Girl,* by Anne Frank: Anne's story of living in Amsterdam, hiding from the Nazis, has resonated with readers young and old since it was first published.

㉘ *Autumn Winifred Oliver Does Things Different,* by Kristin O'Donnell Tubb: Eleven-year-old Autumn Winifred Oliver lives in the tiny settlement of Cades Cove, Tennessee, which will soon become part of Great Smoky Mountains National Park. Autumn's down-to-earth voice reveals the beauty of the mountains, streams, and countryside around her home. Folktales, old-time remedies, and Appalachian superstitions add interest.

㉙ *Bat 6,* by Virginia Euwer Wolff: Just a few years after World War II, the annual Bat 6 girls' softball game is set to celebrate its fiftieth anniversary. A fight breaks out between Shazam, whose father died at Pearl Harbor, and Aki, whose Japanese American family was interred for several years, and the conflict forces the community to look at strong undercurrents of both racism and patriotism.

㉚ *Because of Winn-Dixie,* by Kate DiCamillo: Opal longs to know more about the mother who abandoned her, but her preacher father doesn't want to talk about it. When Opal adopts a lovable mutt she finds at the grocery store, she begins to find ways to fill the void her mother has left.

㉛ *Boy,* by Roald Dahl: Find out where Roald Dahl got his inspiration for the wacky and wicked characters that populate his books when you read these tales from his childhood. You'll read stories of Dahl pulling pranks on candy-store owners and his older sister's fiancé, harrowing accounts of crude-for-today medical procedures, and life inside British boarding schools.

㉜ *Caddie Woodlawn,* by Carol Ryrie Brink: Modeled after the author's grandmother, Caddie is a tomboy who lives in Wisconsin during the mid-1800s. She doesn't want to start acting like a lady, preferring instead to spend time in the woods with her brothers. She's strong and courageous, and she would rather help her dad with chores outside than assist her mother with tasks indoors.

㉝ *Call Me Hope,* by Gretchen Olsen: Even though Hope's mother calls her stupid and makes her feel like everything she does is wrong, she gradually forms a refuge for herself at school and with two women who own a clothing consignment shop. This book shines a light on an issue that isn't talked about much— verbal abuse—while giving us a character who will burrow into our hearts and stay awhile.

㉞ *11 Birthdays,* by Wendy Mass: Amanda and Leo are best friends who have shared birthday celebrations for each of their last ten years. A rift keeps them apart on their eleventh birthday, and they find themselves waking to relive their birthday every day until they find a way to come back together.

㉟ *Ella Enchanted,* by Gail Carson Levine: Ella must always do exactly as she is told, even if she doesn't want to. Can she find a way to break the spell of obedience she suffers under and leave her cruel stepmother and stepsisters for good? This innovatively retold Cinderella story will have you cheering for Ella as she finds out how to rescue herself.

㊱ *Granny Torrelli Makes Soup,* by Sharon Creech: Granny Torrelli ladles up life lessons from her childhood in Italy to help her granddaughter Rosie and Rosie's best friend, Bailey, mend a rift in their friendship.

㊲ *The Graveyard Book,* by Neil Gaiman: A baby orphaned by an attack on his family finds refuge in a graveyard, where he is named Nobody (or Bod, for short) by the long-dead inhabitants. The graveyard's night guardian provides human sustenance, while its ghostly residents teach him how to live.

㊳ *The Green Glass Sea,* by Ellen Klages: Suze and Dewey live in Los Alamos in the final days of World War II, as their parents work on a top-secret "gadget" that will help to win the war. Neither fits in well with other kids in their community, and they don't like each other, either. But when they're forced to spend time together, their relationship grows in ways that neither of them expects.

39. *Heart of a Shepherd,* by Rosanne Parry: Eleven-year-old Ignatius has five older brothers, so everyone calls him Brother. Soon all his brothers and his dad will be away at school or serving in the military. Is he strong enough to help his grandparents run their ranch while everyone else is gone? Topics covered include the importance of family, the church, service to our country, and neighbors pulling together during times of crisis.

40. *The Hermit Thrush Sings,* by Susan Butler: Leora lives in the future after a meteor crashing to Earth changed life as we know it. People are forbidden to leave the village, told by their leaders that birmbas will kill them. When Leora frees a baby birmba trapped in her basement, she embarks on a journey to set it free and discovers the truth about her world.

41. *Julie of the Wolves,* by Jean Craighead George: In her Eskimo village, she is Miyax, but those outside know her as Julie. When she runs away to escape an early, unhappy marriage, she becomes lost on the Alaskan tundra. Will her knowledge of traditional Eskimo ways and help from a pack of wolves lead her to safety?

42. *Masterpiece,* by Elise Broach: An unlikely friendship forms between a lonely young boy named James and a beetle named Marvin. The two are drawn into a staged art heist to recover a long-lost work, and they fall into adventures along the way.

43. *The Mother-Daughter Book Club,* by Heather Vogel Frederick: Four middle-school girls are "forced" by their mothers to join a mother-daughter book club. As they read and go to meetings, they get to know each other beyond the public image they each have at school.

44. *My Louisiana Sky,* by Kimberly Willis Holt: When her grandmother dies, Tiger Ann must decide whether she'll stay with her mentally slow parents in their small Louisiana town, or move in with her glamorous aunt in the big city of Baton Rouge.

45. *Our Only May Amelia,* by Jennifer Holm: May Amelia lives in a remote area of Washington with her six older brothers—it's no wonder she's more a tomboy than a proper young lady. It's 1899, and through May Amelia's eyes we encounter Chinook Indians and logging camps, and get a taste of immigrant life on the frontier.

46. *Rebecca of Sunnybrook Farm,* by Kate Douglas Wiggin: Rebecca's widowed mother sends her away from Sunnybrook Farm to live with her aunts in a village where she can get an education. Even though Rebecca can be troublesome, her winning ways eventually charm even her strictest aunt.

47. *Red Scarf Girl,* by Ji-Li Jiang: The compelling memoir of a girl growing up during the Chinese Cultural Revolution. Ji-Li's authentic voice inspires discussion about family loyalty, government betrayals, and China's history.

48. *Savvy,* by Ingrid Law: Members of Mississippi Beaumont's family gets their "savvy" when they turn thirteen. Her birthday is just days away when her dad lands in the hospital and her mom stays with him. Somehow, she must find her own savvy and bring her family back together. *Savvy* explores issues of family, friendship, budding romance, and the things that are special inside each of us.

49. *Scat,* by Carl Hiaasen: When Nick and Marta's biology teacher doesn't return from a field trip, they suspect foul play. They set out to solve the mystery in the swamp that involves illegal oil drilling, endangered Florida panthers, and other environmental issues.

50. *The Wonderful Wizard of Oz,* by L. Frank Baum: Filled with many adventures of Dorothy Gale and her little dog that you won't find in the movie, this classic is the first in a long series of books about Oz.

BOOKS FOR ELEVEN- TO THIRTEEN-YEAR-OLD READERS

(51) *Al Capone Does My Shirts,* by Gennifer Choldenko: Moose Flanagan left his home, his school, and his baseball team behind in 1935 to move to Alcatraz Island, where his dad was hired as a guard. Now, Moose is working to make new friends and find his place in his family while coming to terms with his sister's severe autism.

(52) *Alligator Bayou,* by Donna Jo Napoli: Sicilian immigrant Calogero finds it difficult to adapt to life in a small Louisiana town in the late 1800s. He's not supposed to socialize with whites or blacks, and tension between the races is building.

(53) *Angus, Thongs and Full-Frontal Snogging,* by Louise Rennison: Fourteen-year-old Georgia worries about her breasts, her looks, and learning how to kiss a boy while dealing with her neurotic cat, clueless parents, and a baby sister still in diapers.

(54) *A Year Down Yonder,* by Richard Peck: Mary Alice has to spend a year away from her Depression-era Chicago home at her grandmother's house in the country. While Grandma is gruff and no-nonsense, she soon enlists Mary Alice in her hilarious schemes to influence neighbors—some friends, some enemies.

(55) *Bloomability,* by Sharon Creech: Thirteen-year-old Dinnie feels abandoned when her parents send her off to live with her aunt and uncle at a boarding school in Switzerland. She learns to love her new home while still holding on to what she loves about the family she left behind.

(56) *Catherine Called Birdy,* by Karen Cushman: Birdy is the witty, irreverent daughter of a minor English nobleman in 1290. Through her diary, we see her repeatedly attempt to quash her father's plans to marry her off.

(57) *The Curse of Addy McMahon,* by Katie Davis: Graphic illustrations interspersed with text tell the story of Addy, who is convinced she suffers from a family curse. But Addy has a lot going right for her, too, and she finds that being open and honest with her friends and family may be all she needs to break her "bad luck."

58 *Dairy Queen,* by Catherine Gilbert Murdock: D. J. has handled much of the work on her family's Wisconsin dairy farm since her dad broke his hip. She's athletic, too, and when she goes out for the high school football team, she sets tongues wagging and gets her normally uncommunicative family members talking.

59 *Everything on a Waffle,* by Polly Horvath: Everyone except Primrose believes her parents are dead and lost at sea. She is shuffled from one guardian to another as she waits for them to return, and hangs out in the local restaurant, where everything is served on a waffle.

60 *Flipped,* by Wendelin Van Draanen: Juli and Bryce have totally different perspectives on the same events. Each chapter flips back and forth between their narratives, as they explore two sides of issues that have occurred since they first met, in second grade. Ultimately, they each find insights into the person they thought they knew.

61 *Framed,* by Frank Cottrell Boyce: Dylan Hughes is the only boy left in Manod, a gray Welsh town with a depressed economy and a dwindling population. When world-famous art arrives there for storage in an old mine, the masterpieces inspire Dylan and the town's eccentric characters to create great changes in themselves and in Manod.

62 *Going Solo,* by Roald Dahl: This memoir of Roald Dahl's early adulthood follows his adventures in Africa and the Mediterranean before and during World War II. Encounters with deadly snakes, lions, and German fighter pilots offer a fascinating glimpse into this time and these places in history.

63 *The Goose Girl,* by Shannon Hale: A richly imagined retelling of the Grimm brothers' classic tale, featuring a heroine who adopts a disguise after an attempt is made on her life. Before she can claim her rightful place in the kingdom, she must gain confidence in her own abilities.

64 *Hattie Big Sky,* by Kirby Larson: Since Hattie's parents died, she has bounced from one relative to another. When an uncle in Montana dies, leaving her his land claim, she finally gets a chance to create a place for herself. But first she has to find out if she can handle the hard life of a homesteader on her own.

65 *Holes,* by Louis Sachar: Stanley Yelnats is wrongly convicted of a crime and sent to dig holes at a reform camp in the desert. To redeem his name, he must enlist the help of the other inmates and break a family curse.

66 *Hoot,* by Carl Hiaasen: Roy is the new kid at a new middle school with new bullies when he sees a boy running outside his bus one day. His curiosity about the boy leads him to make new friends and help save an endangered species.

67 *The House of the Scorpion,* by Nancy Farmer: Ethical issues surrounding human cloning run throughout this narrative, set in a futuristic country created between Mexico and the United States to accommodate the drug trade.

68 *Millions,* by Frank Cottrell Boyce: When a bag of money falls on Damian's cardboard playhouse, he believes it is a gift from God, and that he must give the money to the poor. His brother Anthony would rather invest in real estate, but the bank robber who stole it has other plans.

69 *P.S. Longer Letter Later,* by Paula Danziger and Ann M. Martin. When Tara'Starr moves away from her best friend, Elizabeth, the two keep in touch through letters.

70 *The Princess Diaries,* by Meg Cabot: A Greenwich Village teen discovers she is heir to the throne of a small European country and must learn royal etiquette from her quirky grandmother.

71 *The Secret Garden,* by Frances Hodgson Burnett: Mary is an orphan left mostly to fend for herself in her uncle's English castle. When she discovers her crippled cousin, Colin, she finds a way to bring life back to a hidden garden and the family that has taken her in.

⑦ *The Sisterhood of the Traveling Pants,* by Ann Brashares: An ordinary pair of thrift-store jeans miraculously fits each of four girls, even though they are all different sizes. They take turns wearing the jeans during a summer that turns out to be as magical as the pants.

⑦ *Stargirl,* by Jerry Spinelli: Stargirl turns her school upside down when she enrolls, first repelling kids who consider her a hippie-ish freak, then attracting them with her charmingly weird ways. Leo likes her, but can he stand up to ridicule from his friends?

⑦ *Tangerine,* by Edward Bloor: Paul is legally blind and overshadowed by his football-hero brother. When his family moves to Tangerine County, Florida, Paul rejects his upscale school for one with a poor reputation so he can play soccer. As he discovers more about the accident that blinded him, he turns his town and his family upside down.

⑦ *Uglies,* by Scott Westerfeld: Everyone in Tally's world gets surgery when they turn sixteen to make them beautiful. Tally is nervous and excited as her birthday approaches, but then she meets Shay, who plans to leave for a world outside where people can be themselves. Tally must decide whether to follow Shay and be ugly forever or stay and become pretty.

⑦ *Zlata's Diary,* by Zlata Filipovic: Filipovic was eleven years old when the fighting in her hometown, Sarajevo, started. She kept a diary of her daily life during the conflict there, and we see her thoughts turn from the worries and concerns of a normal preteen to those of a girl who worries for the safety of all she knows.

BOOKS FOR FOURTEEN-YEAR-OLDS TO ADULT READERS

77 *A Certain Slant of Light,* by Laura Whitcomb: Helen died long ago, yet her spirit survives by attaching itself undetected to living humans. James died long ago, too, but he inhabits the body of someone who almost died. As the two get to know each other, they decide to find a way to be together for real.

78 *A Lesson Before Dying,* by Ernest J. Gaines: In southern Louisiana in the 1940s, Jefferson, a black man, is unjustly convicted of murdering a white man and sentenced to die. Unable to find justice, Jefferson's family turns to Grant to help Jefferson find dignity before he goes to the electric chair.

79 *A Northern Light,* by Jennifer Donnelly: A real-life crime story is woven into the fictional tale of Mattie Gokey, whose dying mother asked her to take care of her siblings and her father. But Mattie dreams of college and life as a writer. Stories of lumbering camps, isolated farms, summer camps for wealthy tourists, supply boats, and one-room schoolhouses bring the early-1900s Adirondacks to life.

80 *The Absolutely True Diary of a Part-Time Indian,* by Sherman Alexie: Arnold Spirit leaves high school on the Spokane Indian Reservation for a nearby white school. While he feels like a traitor to his family and friends, he knows he must break through the poverty, alcoholism, and despair that afflict so many people he knows. Can he follow his dreams without denigrating those he leaves behind?

81 *The Adoration of Jenna Fox,* by Mary E. Pearson: Jenna wakes up from a yearlong coma with no memory of her past life. As she pieces her history back together, she discovers the truth about her accident and the price she has paid to go on living. This futuristic mystery addresses issues of scientific and medical ethics.

82 *An Abundance of Katherines,* by John Green: Colin has had nineteen girlfriends named Katherine. While on a summer road trip with his friend, he creates a plan to study the reasons they have all broken up with him, then apply a mathematic formula to find out the length of any future relationships he has.

83 *The Book Thief,* by Markus Zusak: Death narrates the story of nine-year-old Liesel, who lives with her foster family outside Munich in Nazi Germany. She encounters book burnings, Hitler-youth meetings, Jews marching through the streets, food rationing, and Allied bombings, yet books help her endure.

84 *Ender's Game,* by Orson Scott Card: Ender is a rare third child in a future society. He is sent to Battle School to learn to defeat the Buggers that threaten our world.

85 *Every Crooked Pot,* by Renée Rosen: Nina's strawberry birthmark brings her both good and bad attention. She struggles to fit in socially, sure that her birthmark is why she's not popular. Nina's father, Artie, dominates her family life, as everyone around him tries to live up to his high expectations.

86 *Girlwood,* by Claire Dean: When her older sister, Bree, disappears into the woods one night, Polly believes she's hiding nearby to heal her out-of-control life. Polly is certain that Bree is near a magical clearing she calls Girlwood, and she leaves food, clothing, and healing plants to help Bree survive until she's ready to return.

87 *The Good Earth,* by Pearl S. Buck: Wang Lung is a farmer who loves the land and marries O-Lan, a plain-faced hard worker who bears him sons. As his land and wealth increase, Wang Lung turns from the very things that made him successful to grasp at things that cannot make him happy.

88 *Hope Was Here,* by Joan Bauer: Hope works as a waitress wherever her aunt Addie works as a cook. The two have moved around a lot, but their latest job, at a diner in a small town in Wisconsin, may finally be in a place where they can both settle and put down roots.

89 *The Adventures of Huckleberry Finn,* by Mark Twain: When Huck fakes his own death to escape his abusive father, he runs into Jim, an escaped slave. The two of them have many adventures as they raft downriver to find freedom for Jim.

90 *I Capture the Castle,* by Dodie Smith: Two girls are living with their father, stepmother, and brother in a ruined castle in England. When two American men inherit their grandfather's estate down the road, it affects the girls' lives in unforeseen ways.

91 *Impossible,* by Nancy Werlin: Lucy is almost seventeen when she discovers a curse that leaves all the women in her family pregnant, insane, and abandoning their children when they are her age. With the help of her foster parents and her friend Zach, Lucy must find a way to break the curse before it comes true for her.

92 *Light Years,* by Tammar Stein: Maya leaves Israel for college in the United States, but she can't shake the feeling that she is responsible for her boyfriend's death by a suicide bomber. Her story alternates between both countries, highlighting the distances between the two cultures.

93 *Movie Girl,* by Christina Hamlett: Laurie has been chosen to write a screenplay for a film her school will produce. This is the perfect chance for her to attract Artie, the senior heartthrob who doesn't know she exists, by making him the star of the show.

94 *North of Beautiful,* by Justina Chen Headley: Terra Cooper wants to escape her small-town life, in which her true self is as carefully concealed as the port wine–stain birthmark on her face. Terra's journey of self-discovery helps her find the true meaning of beauty and trust in herself.

95 *Pride and Prejudice,* by Jane Austen: Mr. and Mrs. Bennett hope to marry their five daughters well, even though they have only a modest income. Enter an aristocratic neighbor and his friend, Mr. Darcy, and the girls' prospects look up. But first, both Elizabeth Bennett and Mr. Darcy must overcome their pride and prejudice.

96 *The Secret Life of Bees,* by Sue Monk Kidd: Lily runs from her abusive father and finds shelter with August and her sisters. Lily hopes to find out about her long-dead mother, as well as find a place she can call home, but in 1960s South Carolina, racial barriers prevent a white child from living with black women.

97 *Songs for a Teenage Nomad,* by Kim Culbertson: Callie has always moved from town to town with her mom. When she starts high school in a new place, Callie dares to make friends and hope that this time will be different. Then she finds out her mom is keeping a secret about their past and Callie's father.

98 *Speak,* by Laurie Halse Anderson: Everyone at Melinda's high school is angry at her because she called the police to an end-of-summer party. At first, Melinda doesn't say what happened to her that night, or why she barely speaks now. But as the year moves along, she finds her voice through art, and the strength to confront her attacker.

99 *Torched,* by April Henry: Ellie's parents are aging hippies arrested by the FBI for growing marijuana. When Ellie agrees to infiltrate an eco-terrorist group for the FBI in exchange for her parents' freedom, she begins to see good and bad in both organizations.

100 *West with the Night,* by Beryl Markham: As a child growing up in Africa, Beryl Markham faced down lions and wild boar. As an adult, she trained racehorses, learned to fly airplanes, and became a bush pilot, eventually becoming the first pilot to fly solo west with the night, crossing the Atlantic Ocean from Europe to North America.

APPENDIX III
CROWD-PLEASING RECIPES

MAIN DISHES

Show-Ling's Chinese Dumplings

Show-Ling Shyng, PORTLAND, OREGON

This amount is enough to serve our family of five and leave a bit extra. You can double or triple it for more.

- 1 lb. ground pork (you can also use ground beef, chicken, or turkey)
- 1/3–1/2 small bag of prewashed baby spinach (you can substitute other vegetables of your liking)
- 3–4 heads green onion
- 1 small piece ginger root, peeled
- 2 Tbsp. cilantro (for sauce)
- garlic (for sauce)
- salt and peppers to taste
- 1/4 tsp. sesame oil
- 2–3 Tbsp. vegetable oil
- 1–2 packages of dumpling wraps (do *not* get the thick style)

TO MAKE DUMPLINGS:

Chop spinach, green onion, and ginger in a food processor. Combine with ground meat in a big bowl. Add vegetable oil, salt, pepper, and sesame oil; mix well with a spatula. Place some stuffing in the middle of the wrap (make sure to thaw out the wraps ahead of time if they are frozen; microwaving them is *not* recommended). Make sure you don't overstuff the wrap. Apply water to the edge of the wrap and seal the edge by folding one side over the other. It's important to make sure that the seal is tight.

Have a large pot of boiling water ready. Put the dumplings in one by one (you might need to do it in batches). Stir once to make sure that the dumplings are not stuck to the bottom of the pot—make sure to stir gently so you don't break the dumplings.

Add 1 cup of cold water after the dumplings have begun to boil; repeat 3 times. Take the dumplings out of the pot with a slotted spoon and put them in a bowl. After I take the dumplings out, I rinse them quickly with cold water to prevent them from sticking to each other. You can probably also coat them with some olive oil to prevent sticking.

SAUCE:

Chop a few heads of garlic and the cilantro; mix with some soy sauce, sesame oil, and a bit of water. Add vinegar and chili sauce (optional). After serving the dumplings, you can pour the sauce over them or dip them in the sauce.

Serves: 6

Jayne's Chicken Enchilada Casserole

Jayne Mitchell, LAKE OSWEGO, OREGON

- 4 chicken breasts
- 2 cans cream of celery soup
- 1 4-oz. can diced green chilies
- 1 can Rotel
- ½ tsp. oregano
- ¼ tsp. each cumin, sage, and chili powder

- 2 cloves garlic, minced
- 1 lb. cheddar or longhorn cheese
- ¼ lb. Monterey jack cheese (I am lazy, so I just buy the pre-grated, mixed cheese)
- 1 lg. onion, chopped
- 1 pkg. corn tortillas

Sprinkle chicken with salt and pepper and wrap in foil. Bake at 350° for about 30 minutes. Reserve any liquid. Let chicken cool, then tear into pieces.

Add reserved chicken stock to soup and combine with seasonings, chilies, chicken, cheese, and onions (reserve some cheese and onions to sprinkle over the top).

Grease a 9 x 13 x 2–inch casserole dish. Alternate layers of tortillas and soup mixture. Finish with soup mixture, then sprinkle with cheese and onions. Bake at 375° for 35–45 minutes. Let sit 10 minutes before serving. Recipe can be doubled or tripled for bigger groups.

Serves: 6

My Mother's Chili

Christina Katz, WILSONVILLE, OREGON

I've been making and eating this easy chili recipe since I was a kid. This version is not very spicy, so feel free to add spice to suit your family's tastes.

- 3 Tbsp. vegetable oil
- 1 large onion, chopped
- 1 large green bell pepper, chopped
- 1 lb. ground beef
- 2½ cups chopped tomatoes
- 1 can Campbell's tomato soup
- ½ tsp. paprika
- 1 Tbsp. chili powder
- 1 clove garlic, minced

- 1 tsp. salt
- ⅛ tsp. cayenne
- 1 bay leaf
- 2½ cups canned kidney beans, drained

Brown the pepper, onion, and ground beef. Add all remaining ingredients except the beans, and simmer for 1 hour. Add the beans, boil, and serve.

Makes enough to fill a large pot halfway. Double the recipe for bigger crowds. Serve with a dollop of sour cream and shredded sharp cheddar on top. Goes well with cornbread or tortilla chips. Enjoy!

Serves: 4

Cindy's Jambalaya

Cindy Hudson, PORTLAND, OREGON

- 1 whole chicken, cut into pieces (I sometimes use chicken thighs and legs)
- 1 medium onion, chopped
- 1 cup green bell pepper, chopped
- 1 cup celery, chopped
- 1 small can chopped tomatoes
- 4 cups chicken broth
- 1 lb. smoked sausage, andouille sausage, or chopped ham
- 3 cups rice, uncooked
- salt and pepper to taste

Season chicken with salt, black pepper, and cayenne pepper. Brown it on both sides in a little oil in a large skillet. Add a little water, cover, and smother until cooked.

In a separate skillet, sauté seasonings. Add salt and pepper to taste. Fry sausage or ham. Combine chicken, seasonings, meat, tomatoes, chicken broth, and rice in skillet. Bring to a boil, then cover and cook on low heat for 25 minutes or until rice is done.

Serves: 6

Korean Beef

Janelle Asai, PORTLAND, OREGON

- 2 Tbsp. dark soy sauce
- 1 Tbsp. light soy sauce
- 4 Tbsp. granulated sugar
- 1 bunch green onions, coarsely chopped
- 1 2-inch piece fresh ginger, peeled and grated
- 10 cloves garlic, minced
- 2 Tbsp. cooking rice wine
- 5 Tbsp. sesame oil
- 2 lbs. beef tenderloin, sliced thin

Mix all seasonings well and add the beef. Marinate for 1 hour or more. Broil or grill at medium heat for about 10 minutes.

Serves: 6

Peter's Greek Soup

Sandra Pappas, SUTTON, MASSACHUSETTS

- 2 14½-oz. cans chicken broth
- 1½ cans water
- 2 6-oz. cans shredded chicken
- 1 cup uncooked rice
- salt and pepper to taste
- 1 egg
- 3 Tbsp. lemon juice

Bring chicken broth and water to boil; add canned, shredded chicken and rice. Cook about 30 minutes on low heat, until rice is cooked. Drain rice and chicken in strainer over bowl, to catch remaining broth. Set broth aside.

Beat egg and lemon juice together. Strain mixture into separate bowl, then beat into reserved broth. Serve by ladling rice and chicken into a bowl and adding broth on top.

Increase this recipe by adding ¾ of a can of water, 1 can of chicken, and ½ cup of rice for each additional can of chicken broth. Great to serve with crackers or bread.

Serves: 4

Karen's Lasagna

Karen Gotting, PORTLAND, OREGON

Prepared spaghetti sauce and pregrated cheese make this easy to assemble. I don't remember when or why I started adding the spinach, but it adds color and seems healthier. I like to serve it with warm foccacia bread and a green salad. You can make it the night before and heat it up.

- 1 lb. lean ground beef
- 1 onion, chopped
- 2 Tbsp. minced garlic
- 1 jar prepared spaghetti sauce
- 9 lasagna noodles
- 16 oz. ricotta cheese
- 1 egg
- 1 tsp. nutmeg
- 1 10-oz. package frozen chopped spinach
- 1 lb. shredded mozzarella cheese
- ¼ cup grated parmesan cheese

Preheat oven to 375°. Brown ground beef, onion, and garlic over medium heat until cooked through. Drain any fat. Stir in spaghetti sauce; simmer while cooking noodles, stirring occasionally.

Bring a large pot of water to a boil. Cook lasagna noodles in boiling water 8–10 minutes. Drain noodles; rinse with cold water.

Microwave frozen spinach 3–5 minutes, until thawed; drain and press out excess liquid.

In a mixing bowl, combine ricotta cheese with egg, nutmeg, and drained spinach. Set aside ½ cup of meat sauce. To assemble, spread ⅓ of remaining meat sauce in the bottom of a 9 x 13–inch baking dish. Arrange 3 noodles lengthwise over meat sauce. (Noodles will not cover sauce completely; leave a little space in between each noodle.) Spread with half the ricotta cheese mixture. Top with ⅓ of the mozzarella cheese. Repeat layers, ending with third layer of noodles. Top with reserved meat sauce and remaining mozzarella and parmesan cheese.

Cover with foil. Bake in preheated oven for 25 minutes. Remove foil and bake an additional 25 minutes. Cool for 15 minutes before serving.

Serves: 6–8

Mom's Baked Macaroni and Cheese

Henny Hall, CHULA VISTA, CALIFORNIA

- 1 lb. rotini pasta
- 6 Tbsp. margarine or butter
- 3 Tbsp. flour
- 3 cups milk
- 2 tsp. salt
- Ground pepper to taste
- 1½ tsp. dried mustard
- 2 tsp. dried minced onion
- 3 cups shredded sharp cheddar cheese
- ⅓ cup plain bread crumbs

Bring large pot of salted water to a boil and cook pasta until tender. Drain and set aside.

Meanwhile, melt margarine or butter in saucepan. Blend in flour. Add milk slowly and cook, stirring until thickened. Blend in salt, pepper, mustard, and onion. Pour sauce over pasta, along with 2 cups cheese, and mix gently.

Turn into buttered 3-quart casserole dish, sprinkle with remaining cheese and bread crumbs. At this point, the casserole dish can be covered and refrigerated until later in the day or the next day. When ready to eat, bake uncovered in 350° oven, 35–45 minutes, until bubbly and lightly browned.

Serves 8. This recipe can be doubled to feed a crowd.

Catherine's Red Beans and Rice

Catherine Blanchard, BRUSLY, LOUISIANA

- 1 lb. red beans, picked and washed
- 1 lb. smoked pork sausage
- ¼ cup vegetable oil
- 1 medium onion, chopped
- 1 medium green bell pepper, chopped
- 3 cloves garlic, chopped
- Salt, black pepper, and cayenne pepper to taste

Soak the washed beans overnight in a 4-quart pot. In the same soaking water, bring beans to a boil. Add onion, garlic, and bell pepper. Lower heat and simmer about 1½ hours. Add sausage and oil. Simmer 1½ hours longer, occasionally mashing beans with a spoon against the side of the pot to make them creamier.

Serve over cooked rice.

Serves: 8–10

Ellen's Shepherd's Pie

Ellen Hall Saunders, PORTLAND, OREGON

- 4 large potatoes, peeled and cut into a few pieces
- 2 Tbsp. butter
- 1 lb. string beans, washed and tips cut off
- 3 Tbsp. olive oil
- ½ onion, chopped
- 2–3 carrots, chopped
- 2 lbs. ground beef or lamb

- 2–3 zucchini, chopped
- 1 cup canned tomato sauce
- ⅓ cup ketchup
- 2–3 Tbsp. Worcestershire sauce, to taste
- 1 tsp. dried thyme
- 1 tsp. dried marjoram
- 1 Tbsp. soy sauce
- 1 tsp. granulated sugar
- Salt and pepper
- Grated parmesan cheese

Put the potato pieces in a pot, cover with water, add salt, and simmer until the potatoes can be pierced easily with a fork. Drain most of the water, reserving about a cup. Mash the potatoes with salt, pepper, butter, and enough of the reserved water to make them fluffy. Set aside. Steam the green beans in water until just cooked and tender. Drain and set aside.

While the potatoes and green beans are cooking, start the filling. Heat olive oil in a heavy-bottomed sauté pan. Add onions and cook on medium heat until golden brown, about 5 minutes. Add carrots; cook 2 minutes. Add meat and chop with a wooden spoon until meat is separated and browned. If the meat has given off a lot of grease, spoon off as much as possible. Add zucchini; mix. Add tomato sauce, ketchup, Worcestershire sauce, thyme, marjoram, soy sauce, sugar, salt, and pepper. Cook about 15 minutes on low to medium heat until sauce has cooked down and is shiny. You don't want the meat to be very dry, but the sauce shouldn't be very watery, either. If sauce is too dry, add a little water to keep the meat moist. Adjust the seasonings to your liking.

When everything is ready, spread the meat in the bottom of a shallow 3- to 4-quart casserole dish. It should be 1 inch deep or more. Lay the green beans in a layer on top of the meat. Then gently spread the mashed potatoes on top, all the way out to the edges, to make a crust. You can use a fork to make crisscross designs on the top. Sprinkle with parmesan.

The pie can be refrigerated until later in the day or the next day. When ready to eat, put in a 350° oven and heat until top is slightly browned and filling is bubbling. Enjoy with a salad and fruit. This recipe is very forgiving: Adjust the seasoning and the vegetables to your taste or what you have on hand, or add an extra pound of meat and another potato if you need to feed more people.

Serves: 10–12

DESSERTS AND OTHER TREATS

Lisa's Banana Bars

Lisa Willke, PORTLAND, OREGON

- 2 cups flour (I use half whole wheat flour)
- 2 tsp. baking powder
- ½ tsp. salt
- 6 Tbsp. butter or margarine, softened
- ⅔ cup granulated sugar
- ⅔ cup brown sugar
- 1 tsp vanilla
- 4 bananas, mashed
- 1 egg
- 1 cup semisweet chocolate mini-morsels

Preheat oven to 350°. Grease a 10 x 15–inch jelly roll pan (or you can use a 9 x 13–inch pan—the bars will just be thicker). Beat butter, sugars, and vanilla in a large bowl until creamy. Beat in bananas and egg. Gradually beat in flour mixture; stir in morsels. Spread in pan. Bake 20–30 minutes or until a wooden toothpick comes out clean.

Serves: 12

Gingersnaps

FROM AUTHOR *Heather Vogel Frederick* AND HER BOOK
THE VOYAGE OF PATIENCE GOODSPEED

- ¾ cup vegetable shortening
- 1⅓ cup sugar
- 1 egg
- ¼ cup molasses
- 2 tsp. baking soda
- 2 cups flour
- ¼ tsp. salt
- 1 tsp. cinnamon
- 1 tsp. ground cloves
- 1 tsp. ground ginger
- Extra sugar to roll cookies in

Preheat oven to 350°. Cream the shortening and sugar together. Add the remaining ingredients and blend together. Chill the dough for at least 1 hour.

Form small balls with dough and roll them in sugar, then place them on a cookie sheet about 2–3 inches apart. Bake at 350° for 10–12 minutes. Enjoy!

Makes 2 dozen

Laural's Butter Berry Scones

Laural Ringler, BELLINGHAM, WASHINGTON

My houseful of readers enjoys these every Saturday morning; we think they go well with discussing books. Plus, many characters eat scones. For my daughter, that means the animals of Brian Jacques' *Redwall* series. For my son, scones bring to mind the Englishman Arthur Dent, from Douglas Adams' *Hitchhiker's Guide to the Galaxy* series.

- 8 Tbsp. butter
- 1 cup plain yogurt
- 2 Tbsp. brown sugar

- 2 eggs
- 1 cup whole wheat flour
- 2½ cups white flour
- 1 tsp. baking powder
- 1 tsp. baking soda
- ½ teaspoon salt
- ¾ cup frozen raspberries
- ½ cup walnut pieces (optional)

Melt butter in the microwave in a medium-size glass bowl or a 2-cup glass measuring cup. (If you have the latter, you can use the measuring lines when spooning in the yogurt.) Add yogurt, brown sugar, and eggs; stir together.

In a bread or pasta-serving bowl (at least 12 inches in diameter, with low sides), stir together dry ingredients. Pour butter mixture over flour mixture and combine gently with a large spoon. Pat dough into the bottom of the bowl, then distribute frozen berries and walnuts onto one side of your dough circle. Preheat oven to 400°.

Use your hands to fold dough over the berries and walnuts, as though you are making an omelet. Using a knife, cut triangles like you're serving pie, though there's no need to cut from the exact center (just close to it). Cut 8 triangles for very large scones, and up to twice that many for smaller scones to have with tea, transferring each to an ungreased baking sheet with the knife under and a hand over it.

Bake 15–20 minutes. The scones are done when slightly browned and not doughy next to the berries. Serve warm, with honey.

Makes 8 large servings or 16 small servings

Julie's Wacky Cake

Julie Peterson, MECHANICSBURG, PENNSYLVANIA

This is an egg-free, dairy-free, chocolate cake recipe called Wacky Cake. It dates back to World War II, when things were rationed. My mom and I used to make it as an after-school snack because it was quick and little. It's great with Cool Whip, whipped cream, or vanilla ice cream. I find myself making it a lot now, since my son has many food allergies.

- 1½ cups flour
- 1 cup sugar
- 1 tsp. salt
- 1 tsp. baking soda
- 4 Tbsp. unsweetened cocoa powder

Sift ingredients into an ungreased 8 x 8–inch cake pan. Add these ingredients one at a time:

- 1 cup water
- 2 Tbsp. vegetable oil
- 2 tsp. vanilla
- 1 tsp. vinegar

Stir with a fork until smooth and creamy. Bake at 350° for 30 minutes.

Serves: 9

Perilee's Wartime Spice Cake

FROM AUTHOR *Kirby Larson* AND HER BOOK *HATTIE BIG SKY*

- 1 cup brown sugar, firmly packed
- 1½ cups water
- ⅓ cup shortening or lard
- ⅔ cup raisins
- ½ tsp. each ground cloves and nutmeg
- 2 tsp. cinnamon
- 1 tsp. baking soda
- 1 tsp. salt

- 2 cups flour
- 1 tsp. baking powder

Boil brown sugar, water, shortening, raisins, and spices together for 3 minutes. Cool. Dissolve baking soda in 2 tsp. water and add with salt to raisin mixture. Stir together flour and baking powder and add to raisin mixture 1 cup at a time, beating well after each addition. Pour into a greased and floured 8-inch square pan and bake at 325° for about 50 minutes.

Serves: 9

(Adapted from Butterless, Eggless, Milkless Cake, in *Recipes and Stories of Early-Day Settlers;* and from Depression Cake, described in *Whistleberries Stirabout Depression Cake: Food Customs and Concoctions of the Frontier West.*)

INDEX

ACKNOWLEDGMENTS

MY THANKS GO out to many people who helped move this book along. Some contributed in small ways, others had larger input, but every contribution helped me to create a more valuable guide.

First, I want to thank the moms and daughters in my two Portland, Oregon, book clubs. My first club, with my daughter Madeleine, was created in 2001 and includes Karen and Kirsten Gotting, Janelle Asai and Emily Hordes, Yasmeen Nazeeri and Sophie Hurst, Jayne and Elisabeth Mitchell, and Jan and Julia Ohman. My second club, with my daughter Catherine, came into existence in 2004 and includes Karen and Alannah Berson, Joan and Liza Overholser, Ellen and Franny Saunders, Show-Ling Shyng and Jaeda Patton, and Lisa and Monica Willke. Our wonderful, sometimes trying, but invaluable times together over the years have made me believe in the life-changing experience of being in a mother-daughter book club.

In addition to the moms in my own book clubs, moms in other mother-daughter book clubs from around the country generously shared their experiences with me. The advice in this book is richer because of their stories about forming their groups, innovative activities they scheduled with their daughters over the years, and how they solved problems. My thanks go out to everyone who gave input: Audrey Banks from Gaithersburg, Maryland; Lisa Bany-Winters from Glenview, Illinois; Jill Beres from Falls Church, Virginia; Ellen Calves from Goshen, New

York; Carrie Chute from Bellingham, Washington; Gina Davis from St. Peters, Missouri; Eileen Faradji from Miami, Florida; Sheila Ferry from Bellevue, Washington; Mindy Foley from Lexington, Kentucky; Maria Gallardo from Woodcliff Lake, New Jersey; Emma Gilleland from Portland, Oregon; Melissa Halloran from St. Peters, Missouri; Julie Heeg from Brookfield, Wisconsin; Kate Levin from New York, New York; Wendie Lubic from Washington, D.C.; Denise Neary from Rockville, Maryland; Lisa Newman from Bethel Park, Pennsylvania; Tamie Osterloh from Council Bluffs, Iowa; Julie Peterson from Mechanicsburg, Pennsylvania; Inez Renterria from Phoenix, Arizona; Marci Rosenthal from Canton, Massachusetts; Lesly Weiner from New York, New York; and Heather Yano from Ledyard, Connecticut.

Christina Katz, my friend and writing mentor, first inspired me to think of writing a book about mother-daughter book clubs. There's so much to thank Christina for, including her vision, help with many drafts of my book proposal, advice on how to reach out to my audience, and introduction to her agent. Now also my agent, Rita Rosenkranz has given me valuable encouragement and advice along the way. Thanks also to my editor, Brooke Warner, at Seal Press. She liked the idea of *Book by Book* from the beginning and found a way to translate it into print.

Members of my writers' group listened patiently as I read chapters out loud. Deanna Hyland and John Axford provided great feedback, and Ellen Saunders went above and beyond by reading the whole manuscript and giving welcome suggestions.

Of course, without my two lovely daughters, Madeleine and Catherine, I would never have created even one mother-daughter book club. Their love of reading and our reading together over the years have given me insights into their lives and an appreciation for the wonderful people they continue to become. I cherish every moment we have spent together as part of our groups. And immeasurable thanks go to my husband, Randy, my foremost cheerleader, who not only encourages me to keep pushing myself and growing, but also provides the support and love I need to make it happen.

ABOUT THE AUTHOR

CINDY HUDSON nourished her love of reading as a young girl while wandering among the shelves of her public library, a converted Victorian home of cubbyhole rooms filled with books in Plaquemine, Louisiana. She is still happiest exploring the aisles of her local library and bookstores every-where. She is also thrilled to have a husband and two daughters who share her passion for books and the worlds they open up. Hudson writes from her home in Portland, Oregon. Visit her online at www.motherdaughterbookclub.com.

Author Cindy Hudson with her daughters, Catherine and Madeleine

Selected Titles from Seal Press

For more than thirty years, Seal Press has published groundbreaking books. *By women. For women.*

Visit our website at www.sealpress.com. Check out the Seal Press blog at www.sealpress.com/blog.

Real Girl Real World: A Guide to Finding Your True Self, by Heather M. Gray and Samantha Phillips. $15.95, 1-58005-133-2. In this fun and essential guide, real girls share their experiences, showing that there's no one "right" way to navigate the twisting road of adolescence.

Gringa: A Contradictory Girlhood, by Melissa Hart. $16.95, 1-58005-294-0. This coming-of-age memoir offers a touching, reflective look at one girl's struggle with the dichotomies of class, culture, and sexuality.

It's a Boy: Women Writers on Raising Sons, edited by Andrea J. Buchanan. $14.95, 1-58005-145-6. Seal's edgy take on what it's really like to raise boys, from toddlers to teens and beyond.

It's a Girl: Women Writers on Raising Daughters, edited by Andrea J. Buchanan. $14.95, 1-58005-147-2. The companion title to *It's a Boy,* this anthology describes what it's like—and why it's a unique experience—to mother girls.

Reclaiming Our Daughters: What Parenting a Pre-Teen Taught Me About Real Girls, by Karen Stabiner. $14.95, 1-58005-213-9. Offers a message of hope and optimism to the parents of adolescent and pre-adolescent girls.

The Stay-at-Home Survival Guide: Field-Tested Strategies for Staying Smart, Sane, and Connected When You're Raising Kids at Home, by Melissa Stanton. $14.95, 1-58005-247-9. The essential how-to book for stay-at-home mothers, written by a media-savvy former "working mom".